RXpert SERIES
Student's Companion

Industrial Pharmacy

A Practical Manual

Rxpert SERIES Student's Companion

Industrial Pharmacy

A Practical Manual

Noopur Verma
School of Pharmaceutical Sciences
(Formerly University Institute of Pharmacy),
CSJM University (Formerly Kanpur University),
Kanpur.

Ajay Kumar Gupta
School of Pharmaceutical Sciences
(Formerly University Institute of Pharmacy),
CSJM University (Formerly Kanpur University),
Kanpur.

Shweta Patel
Hygia Institute of Pharmaceutical
Education & Research, Lucknow

™ **PharmaMed Press**
An Imprint of BSP Books Pvt. Ltd.
4-4-309/316, Giriraj Lane,
Sultan Bazar, Hyderabad - 500 095.

Industrial Pharmacy: A Practical Manual

by **Noopur Verma, Ajay Kumar Gupta and Shweta Patel**

Published by

PharmaMed Press

An Imprint of BSP Books Pvt. Ltd.

4-4-309/316, Giriraj Lane, Sultan Bazar, Hyderabad - 500 095.

Phone: 040-23445688; Fax: 91+40-23445611

E-mail: info@pharmamedpress.com

www.pharmamedpress.com/pharmamedpress.net

ISBN: 978-93-49562-24-0 (Hardback)

Dr. N.K. Jain
M.Pharm., Ph.D., LL.M., F.I.C
Professor of Pharmaceutics
Cell 9425170897, 8770988500

Ex Head
Department of Pharmaceutical Sciences
Dr. H.S. Gour Central University
SAGAR 470003 INDIA
Ex Emeritus Fellow *[U.G.C.]*
Rajiv Gandhi Technological University
BHOPAL 462033 INDIA

Forward

It is my pleasure to introduce "A Practical Handbook of Industrial Pharmacy" book to undergraduate and graduate pharmacy students of all Indian universities. This book is a comprehensive guide that covers the syllabus prescribed by the Pharmacy Council of India (PCI), New Delhi. The book has been written with special emphasis on the practical aspects of industrial pharmacy. It is divided into 15 chapters, each dedicated to relevant topics related to industrial pharmacy.

The authors have done an excellent job of presenting the material in a clear and concise manner. The book is well-organized, making it easy for students and teaches as well to find the relevant information they need, illustrated with the help of clear diagrams. The authors have also put their efforts to support the readers to understand the concepts of prescribed industrial pharmacy practical by providing searching questions and answers.

I am confident that this book would serve as an invaluable resource to the students of pharmacy and professionals in the field of industrial pharmacy, which is difficult to apprehend due to the obvious gap in theory and practice. I would like to congratulate the authors on their outstanding contribution and wish them all the best for their future endeavors.

11 November 2024

Prof. N.K. Jain
Ex- Professor & Head
Department of Pharmaceutical Sciences
Dr. H.S. Gour University
SAGAR [M.P.] 470001

Preface

The field of Industrial Pharmacy plays a pivotal role in the pharmaceutical industry, bridging the gap between academic, drug discovery and the production of safe and effective pharmaceutical products. This practical manual, "Industrial Pharmacy – A Practical Manual," is designed in accordance with the latest PCI syllabus for the Bachelor of Pharmacy (B. Pharm) program. It aims to provide students with hands-on experience and a deeper understanding of various essential pharmaceutical formulations and quality control processes.

This book covers a wide range of practical exercises that are crucial for the preparation and evaluation of pharmaceutical products. Beginning with preformulation studies on commonly used drugs like Paracetamol and Aspirin, students are guided through the formulation and evaluation of tablets and capsules, including techniques such as film coating. The book also delves into the preparation of sterile products like injections and ophthalmic formulations, which are critical in clinical practice.

Additionally, students will engage in quality control testing as per the Indian Pharmacopoeia (IP), enhancing their knowledge of regulatory standards and ensuring that the products they develop meet stringent safety and efficacy requirements. The preparation of topical formulations like creams, and the evaluation of packaging materials such as glass containers, further provide a comprehensive learning experience. For a strong foundation of the theory of Industrial Pharmacy the authors recommend 'Industrial Pharmacy I' and 'Industrial Pharmacy II' books (published by M/s Vallabh Prakashan, Delhi) both authored by the internationally renowned academician, Professor N. K. Jain.

This practical manual is intended to serve as a practical guide, enabling students to apply knowledge in real-world scenarios and fostering the skills necessary for a successful career in the pharmaceutical industry. We hope this manual will be a valuable resource for both students and educators, contributing to the development of skilled professionals in the field of pharmaceutical sciences.

Acknowledgement

We would like to express our sincere gratitude to the Pharmacy Council of India (PCI), New Delhi, for prescribing the syllabus that this book covers. We would also like to thank the readers and publisher for their interest in "A Practical Handbook of Industrial Pharmacy". We hope that this book will serve as an invaluable resource for students of pharmacy and professionals in the field of industrial pharmacy.

This milestone was achieved with the help of many individuals, both directly and indirectly. We are grateful for the honest efforts of our team and the support of many wonderful people, including Prof. (Dr.) Pramod Yeole, Prof. N.K. Jain, Prof. P.K. Sahoo, Prof. Gajendra Singh, Dr. Vivek Verma (IIT, Kanpur), Dr. A. Rajendiran, Dr. Jyoti Nanda, and Dr. Anju Singh. We would also like to thank the Honorable Vice Chancellor of CSJM University (formerly Kanpur University), Kanpur, for their constant motivation and support in accomplishing this task.

In addition, we are deeply appreciative of our family members, scholars particularly Sangeeta, Kamya, Prachi, Anmol, Suraj, Dheeraj, and others. The scholars are always the most vital component of any institution of higher learning and education. We take responsibility for any deviations or errors that may have been overlooked, and we would be extremely appreciative if readers would bring them to our attention. Any valuable feedback that could help improve future editions of this book will be greatly appreciated.

We would also like to thank the publishers for their support in bringing this book to fruition. Without their help, this book would not have been possible. Once again, we express our gratitude to everyone who has contributed to this book. We hope that this book will continue to be a valuable resource for years to come.

Contents

CHAPTER 1

PREFORMULATION STUDIES ON PARACETAMOL

Aim: To evaluate the Pre-formulation parameters of Paracetamol drug.

Requirements:

1. **Apparatus required**: Beaker, graduated cylinder, hot air oven, sieve no. 10, test tube, pH meter, funnel, stopwatch, bulk density apparatus, weighing balance, burette stand, thermometer, capillary tube, weighing bottle with stopper, oven, desiccator.
2. **Chemicals required:** Paracetamol, water, ethanol, chloroform

Principle: Preformulation studies provide a framework for the qualitative and quantitative estimation of drug before developing dosage form with /without pharmaceutical ingredients. The aim of Preformulation studies is to develop reliable and competent dosage form, by providing the drug's release kinetic profile, its interaction profile with ingredients and the physiochemical parameters of reported drug.

Need and importance of dosage form:

1. To provide reliable & competent delivery of drug.
2. To enhance self-life of drug.
3. To protect drug from degradation by gastric pH. Example: enteric coated tablet.
4. To suppress the odor and taste of the drug.
5. To enhance solubility and stability, for liquid preparations that are unstable or insoluble.
6. Providing rate-controlling drug action. Example: sustained release and controlled release tablet such as aspirin.

Objectives:

1. Determining the physicochemical properties of drug molecules.
2. Determining the kinetics and stability of reported drug molecules.
3. Compatibility with commonly used excipients.
4. Formulation of dosage form and stability studies.

- **Name of the compound:** Paracetamol
- **Chemical name:** N-acetyl-para-aminophenol
- **Molecular formula:** $C_8H_9NO_2$
- **Molecular weight:** 151.165 g·mol^{-1}
- **Molecular structure:**

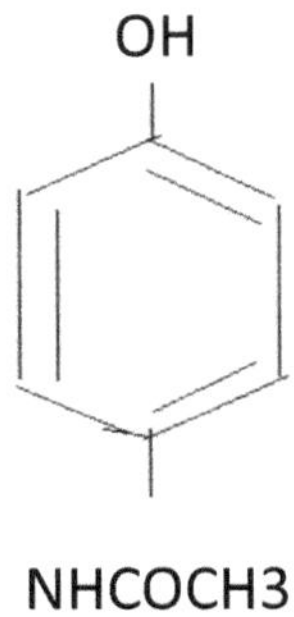

- **Description:** white powder
- **Category:** Nonsteroidal anti-inflammatory drug
- **Dose:** 500 mg
- **Storage:** protected from light and moisture

Preformulation studies/parameters are as follows:

A. Organoleptic properties

B. Bulk characterization

1. Bulk density
2. Hygroscopicity
3. Fine particle characterization
4. Powder flow properties
5. Crystallinity and polymorphism

C. Solubility parameter

1. Ionization constant- pKa
2. pH solubility profile
3. Common ion effect-Ksp
4. Thermal effect
5. Solubilization
6. Partition coefficient
7. Dissolution

D. Stability parameter

1. Stability in toxicology preparation
2. Solution stability
   (a). pH stability
3. Solid state stability
   (a). Bulk stability
   (b). Compatibility

PREFORMULATION STUDIES:

A. Organoleptic Properties:

The organoleptic properties are used for the identification and checking of drug molecules through eye examination method, to compare it with the standards mentioned in the Indian Pharmacopoeia. For identification of sample drug color, odor and taste are observed in day light besides clear background. *Color* may be off-white, cream yellow, tan, shiny. *Odor* may be pungent, sulfurous, fruity, aromatic and odorless. *Taste* may be acidic, bitter, bland, intense, sweet and tasteless.

B. Bulk Characterization:

Particle size, density, shape, and environmental conditions are important parameters that affect the flow characteristics of the sample and the formulation process. Following methods can be used for bulk characterization:

1. Bulk density: The bulk density of a powder is equal to the ratio of the mass of an untapped powder sample and its volume and expressed in gm/ml. It is measured by pouring the weighed sample powder/granules into the graduated cylinder using bulk density apparatus (no tapping is required) (Fig. 1.1), record the reading. and perform same procedure three times. Bulk density is used to determine the amount of powder /granules to fill in a space of blender or hopper for tablet formulation, and calculated by the following formula:

$$D_b = M/Vo$$

Where,

D_b = Bulk Density,

M = Mass of powder,

Vo = Bulk volume of sample powder

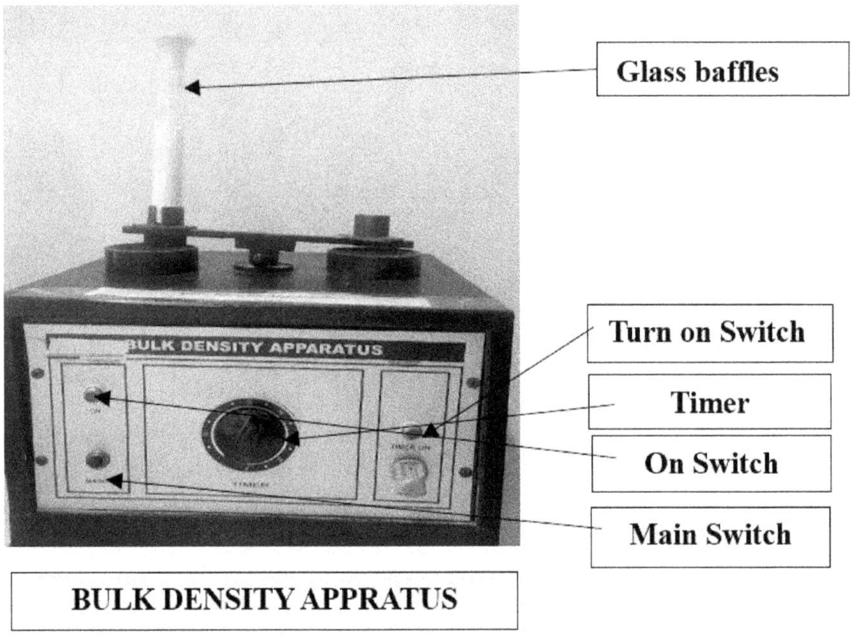

Fig. 1.1 Bulk Density Apparatus.

2. **Tapped density:** To determine the tapped density, a graduated cylinder containing the weighed granules or powder is tapped 100 times using a bulk density apparatus. The minimum volume (Vt) occupied in the cylinder and the weight (m) of the granules/powder are measured and recorded. The tapped density is then calculated using the formula:

$$D_t = M/Vt$$

Where,

M = Mass of powder,

V_t = Tapped volume of powder

3. **Angle of repose:** It is the maximum angle formed between the height of the pile of the powder and the horizontal plane. If, the value of Angle of repose (θ) is large, it indicates irregular shape and rough surface of particle. The lower the value (θ), the better the flow properties. To measure the angle of repose, the test sample is filled into a funnel to the brim (top of the funnel) and allowed to flow downward onto a piece of graph paper.

The cone formed on the graph is taken to measure the surface area of pile by using height of pile and radius of pile, as shown in Fig. 1.2.

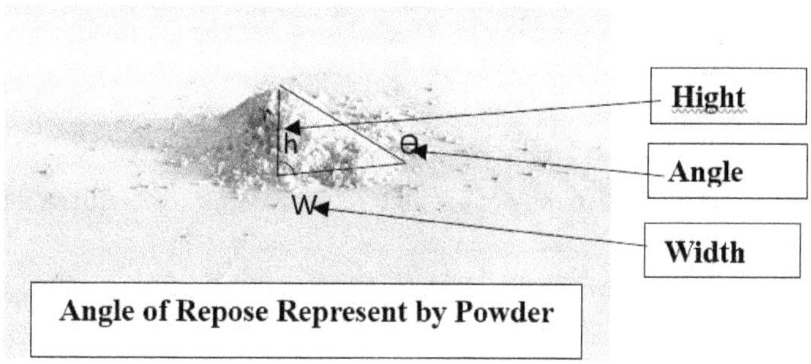

Fig. 1.2 Angle of repose.

Calculate the Angle of repose by the following formula:

$$\theta = \tan^{-1} h/r$$

Where,

Θ = angle of repose

h = height of the powder in cm,

r = radius of heap of powder in cm

Table 1.1 The following are the acceptance criteria for angle of repose.

S. No	Angle of repose (θ)	Type of flow
1.	<25	Excellent
2.	25-30	Good
3.	30-40	Fair/passable
4.	>40	Very poor

4. The Compressibility: It determines the mechanical properties of individual particles of powder or granules, which play an important role in the preparation of tablets.

Compressibility of powder or granule particles can be determined by given methods:

(a) The Hausner's Ratio (Hauser Ratio)

(b) The Carr's compressibility index

(a) Hausner's Ratio: The ratio of the tapped bulk density to the bulk density is known as the Hausner ratio. This ratio serves as a useful cohesiveness indicator since it represents particle friction. Powders with a Hausner ratio greater than 1.4 are considered cohesive and difficult to fluidize. A powder that flows freely is defined by ratios below 1.20. It is calculated by using formula:

$$\text{Hausner's Ratio} = (Dt / Db)$$

Table 1.2 The following are the acceptance requirements for Hausner's ratio.

S. No	Hausner's ratio	Type of flow
1.	1.00–1.11	Excellent
2.	1.12–1.18	Good
3.	1.19–1.25	Fair
4.	1.26–1.34	Passable
5.	1.35–1.45	Very poor
6.	1.46–1.59	Extremely poor

(b) **Carr's Index** It measures the relationship between interparticle interaction and flow property of powder/granules. The higher the Carr's Index value, the greater the difference between bulk and tapped density of sample. Compressibility index of the granules/powder is determined by using the formula:

$$CI\ (\%) = [(Dt - Db / Db)] \times 100$$

Where,

CI = Carr's index

Dt = tapped density of sample

Db = bulk density of sample

Table 1.3 Table of Car's Index as an indication of powder flow properties.

S. No	Carr's index (%)	Type of flow
1.	5-15	Excellent
2.	12-16	Good
3.	18-21	Fair to passable
4.	23-35	Poor
5.	33-38	Very poor
6.	>40	Extremely poor

5. **Hygroscopicity:** Hygroscopicity is a general term used to describe the ability of a substance to absorb moisture from its surrounding without any change in physical state, while " hygroscopic" term refers to

substance that retain moisture. Atmospheric moisture is one of the major factors that affects the chemical stability, flow property and compatibility of ingredients used in pharmaceutical preparation.

The hygroscopicity of drug sample is determined by placing glass plate contain thin layer of weighed/given drug sample in an open container with controlled relative humidity prepared with saturated aqueous salt solution. The amount of moisture absorbed by sample can be determined by Karl-fischer titration, Thermogravimetric analysis (TGA), and Gravimetry method.

6. **Sieve Analysis:** The main aim of sieve analysis is to determine the size distribution of different drug particles present. A series of sieves is arranged in the order of their decreasing sieves numbers i.e 85 #, 60#, 40#, 22#, 16 #, 10# and placed over the shaker. Accurately weigh 100 g of drug and transferred to a sieve no.10# which is kept on the top of the sieves. The sieves are shaken mechanically or electrically for about half an hour. Then the drug retained on each of the sieves are taken, weight separately, and expressed in terms of percentage, is calculated by:

$$\text{\% powder retained} = \frac{\text{Weight of powder that retained on the sieve}}{\text{Weight of total powder taken for experiment}} \times 100$$

C. Solubility Parameter:

Solubility profile is the foundation of preformulation research, which determine effectiveness of drug. Solubility and permeability serve as the cornerstones of the biopharmaceutics classification system. solubility analysis includes, pKa determination, pH solubility profile, partition coefficient.

1. pH: The pH of a solution is an important factor for the solubilization and stability of drug. A solution with a pH of 7 is considered neutral, a pH less than 7 is considered acidic, and a pH greater than 7 is considered basic. The ionic and non-ionic forms of drug depend on the pH of solution. For the measurement of pH, prepare 1% w/v solution of Paracetamol in an appropriate solvent and measure the pH of paracetamol solution using pH meter.

2. Solubility profile in solvent: Solubility are expressed in terms of volume or mass of the solute that dissolves in a given volume or mass of a solvent. In pharmacopoeias, solubility values are expressed as the number of parts by volume of solvent needed to dissolve one part by weight of a solid or one part by volume of a liquid. The solubility of a drug is a crucial physicochemical feature as it influences the drug's bioavailability, release rate into the dissolving medium, and therapeutic efficacy. This is a crucial phase in the formulation-development process. Solubility is determined by using a range of solvents, including ethanol, chloroform, distilled water, and 0.1 M HCL and analysed at 249nm. The solubility of material is determined by making a saturated solution of the material, where excess quantity of drug is taken in 10 mL of each solvent and occasionally stirring for 24 hrs at room temperature. Afterwards the sample is filtered and filtrate is suitably diluted and analysed spectrophotometrically at 249nm.

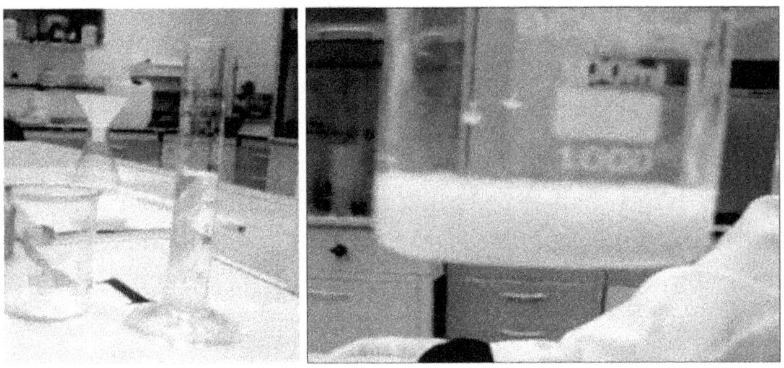

Fig.1.3 Solubility analysis of test drug.

Table 1.4 Solubility criteria as per IP".

S. No	Solubility	Parts of solvent required for 1 part of solute
1.	Very soluble	Less than 1
2.	Freely soluble	1 to 10
3.	Soluble	10 to 30
4.	Sparingly soluble	30 to 100
5.	Slightly soluble	100 to 1000
6.	Very slightly soluble	1000 to 10000
7.	Practically insoluble	10000 or more

3. **pKa Determination**: The solubility of a molecule at a particular pH is determined by its ionization characteristics, or pKA (ionization constant), which can be affected by basic or acidic functional groups. The dissociation constant of a drug that can ionize within a pH range of 1 to 14 must be determined, as pH changes can affect a drug's solubility and, in the meantime, its absorption. The ionized and unionized drug concentration at a given pH can be estimated using the Henderson-

Hasselbach equation.

For acidic compounds: pH = pKa + log [ionized drug] / [un-ionized drug]

For basic compounds: pH = pKa + log [un-ionized drug] / [ionized drug]

Table 1.5 pKa determination table.

S. No	Nature of drug	Ionization	pKa
1.	Very weak acid	Unionized at all pH	> 8
2.	Moderately weak acid	Unionized at gastric pH-1.2	2.5-7.3
3.	Strong acid	Ionize at all pH	< 2.5
4.	Very weak base	Unionize at all pH	<5
5.	Moderately weak base	Unionize at intestinal pH	5-11
6.	Strong base	Ionize at all pH	>11

4. **Partition coefficient**: Partition coefficient is defined as the ratio of un-ionized drug concentrations between the organic and aqueous phases, at equilibrium, where aqueous phase is water and organic phase is octanol. Drug with high partition coefficient will be able to cross the lipid cell membrane.

$$\text{Partition coefficient (Po/w)} = \frac{\text{Concentration of drug in oil phase}}{\text{Concentration of drug in aqueous phase}}$$

D. Stability Studies: Stability of active pharmaceutical ingredient is performed at different temperature and humidity, as per the below table:

Table 1.6 Stability studies.

S. No	Study	Storage condition	Minimum time period covered by data at submission
1.	Long term	25^0 C to 30^0C ± 2 ^{0} C/60 % to 65% RH± 5% RH	12 months
2.	Intermediate	30^0C ± 2 ^{0} C/ 65% RH± 5% RH	6 months
3.	Accelerated	40^0C ± 2 ^{0} C/ 75% RH± 5% RH	6 months

Observation and evaluation tables of Preformulation studies

Organoleptic Properties:

S. No	Test	Specification	Observation
1.	Color	White Crystalline powder	
2.	Odor	Odorless	
3.	Taste	Slightly bitter	

Solubility profile of Paracetamol drug:

S. No	Chemical (Solvent)	Specification	Observation
1.	Water	Sparingly soluble in water	
2.	Alcohol	Freely soluble in alcohol	
3.	Acetone	Freely soluble in alcohol	
4.	Ether	Very slightly soluble	

Solubility profile in different solvents:

S. No	Chemical (solvent)	Absor bance	Dilution factor	Concentrati on(mg/mL)	Solubility observed as (partsrequired to dissolve 1g of drug)
1.	Water			mg/mL	
2.	Ethanol			mg/mL	
3.	0.1 N HCl			mg/mL	
4.	Chloroform			mg/mL	

Result: The Preformulation parameters of the prepared Paracetamol drug were found to be:

S. No	Test	Specification	Observation
1.	Color	white amorphous powder	
2.	Odor	Slightly bitter	
3.	Taste	bitter taste, no distinct odour	
4.	Solubility	Sparingly soluble in water, freely soluble in alcohol, acetone, very slightly, soluble in ether and methylene chloride	

contd..

5.	pH	5.5-6.5	
6.	Bulk density g/ml		
7.	Tapped density g/ml		
8.	Angle of Repose	<25	
9.	Carr's Index	5-15	
10.	Hausner's ratio	1.00-1.11	
11.	Partition coefficient	>1<	

QUESTIONS

Q.1 What are the objective of pre-formulation studies?

Q.2 Why physicochemical estimation of a drug is required?

Q.3 What do you understand by Bulk characterization?

Q.4 What do you understand by 'organoleptic properties'?

Q.5 Define Hygroscopy?

Q.6 Describe techniques used to identify crystalline or amorphous nature of drug?

Q.7 Define 'Density' and its type?

Q.8 What is partition coefficient?

Q.9 Why angle of repose is important in the performulation studies?

Q.10 What is the role of tapped density in drug formulation?

Answers on page.no: 84

CHAPTER 2

FORMULATION OF PARACETAMOL GRANULES FOR TABLETS

Aim: To prepare, evaluate and submit granules for 40 Paracetamol Tablets each containing 500 mg of Paracetamol (IP)

Requirements:

1. **Apparatus required:** Mortar and pestle, graduated measuring cylinder 100ml & 250ml, beaker, sieve no.# 10, #22, #44, #60, hot air oven, dryer
2. **Chemical required:** Paracetamol, lactose, dry starch, magnesium stearate, talc

Theory:

Granulation is the unit operations which play an important role in the production of solid dosage form i.e. tablet and capsules. Tablets are the compressed solid unit dosage form prepared either by direct compression or after making granules of active pharmaceutical ingredient and excipient by agglomeration or granulation techniques. Granulation is a process in which powder particles are made to bind each other results in agglomeration of particles called granules. Excipients used in the granulation process such as binder (starch), disintegrating agent (starch), diluent (lactose), lubricant (Magnesium stearate), glidant (talc) provide sufficient moisture, hardness, and density in the compressed tablets. Granulation ensures the uniformity of drug in the final product.

Compressed tablets are prepared by three type of granulation methods:

1. Wet granulation method
2. Dry granulation method
3. Direct granulation method

The wet granulation method is the considered method for preparing compressed tablets add provide better surface modification, appearance, and compression of granules.

Following steps involved in wet granulation method:

(a) Weighing and blending of ingredients in geometrical order

(b) Preparation of damp mass by adding binding agents

(c) Converting the damp mass into wet granules with the help sieve

(d) Drying of granules

(e) Sieving to obtain uniform granule size

(f) Addition of lubricant

(g) Compression of tablet

Paracetamol as API:

Paracetamol is a NASIDs, commonly used to treat fever and mild to moderate pain. Paracetamol is categorized in class 1 (highly soluble and highly permeable), off white in color with chemical formula $C_8H_9NO_2$, and amorphous in nature. Paracetamol tablets are prepared by using paracetamol as API (antipyretic), lactose as adjuvant, dry starch as binder, starch monohydrate as disintegrating agent, magnesium stearate as lubricant and talc as glidant.

Standards (IP): Paracetamol tablets contain not less than 95.0% and not more than 105.0% of the stated amount of Paracetamol, $C_8H_9NO_2$

PREPARATION OF PARACETAMOL TABLETS

Table 2.1 Paracetamol tablets formulation table.

S. No	Ingredients	1 tablet(mg)	For 40 tablets(gm)
1.	Paracetamol	125	
2.	Lactose	375	
3.	Dry starch	48	
4.	Talc	40	
5.	Magnesium stearate	12	
6.	Starch monohydrate.	q.s.	

q.s. = Quantity sufficient

A. Preparation of granules:

1. **Preparation of granulating medium (10% starch paste):** Weigh 10 g of dry starch and transfer into a beaker of 250ml. To this add 50ml water and make slurry with continuous stirring, then add 25 ml of water in to the starch slurry and place it on a wire gauge. Heat the slurry to obtain a thick paste. Add the remaining 25 ml of water to the slurry with continuous stirring. Stop heating when starch mucilage gets formed, cool starch paste.
2. Weigh prescribed quantity of disintegrating (starch monohydrate) and lubricating (magnesium stearate) agents, pass through sieve no. 60# and divide into two equal parts, first part will be added during wet granulation and second part add after in-dried granules.
3. For wet granulation, weigh the required quantity of paracetamol, lactose and pass through sieve no. 60#, blend together with first part of lubricating and disintegrating agent as mention in step 2.
4. Add starch paste to the above mixture little by little with continuous kneading by hand, so that uniform damp mass or wet mass is formed.
5. The wet mass is forced to pass through a sieve no. 60# or 80#.
6. Dry the wet granules at in the oven for one hr by spreading them in a tray.
7. Dried granules are passed through sieve no. 16# or 10# and mixed with second part of the disintegrating agent and lubricant.
8. compress the granules to prepare the tablet.

B. Punching of tablet:

1. Weigh the granules equivalent to 500 mg of paracetamol (i.e. about 2.40 g of prepared granules).
2. Set the table punching machine.
3. Fill weighed granules into the die cavity.
4. Apply optimum pressure on upper punch to compress the granules.
5. After compression, eject prepared tablets and check for desired hardness with hardness tester.
6. If the tablet has sufficient hardness, then repeat the procedure to prepare the next tablet.

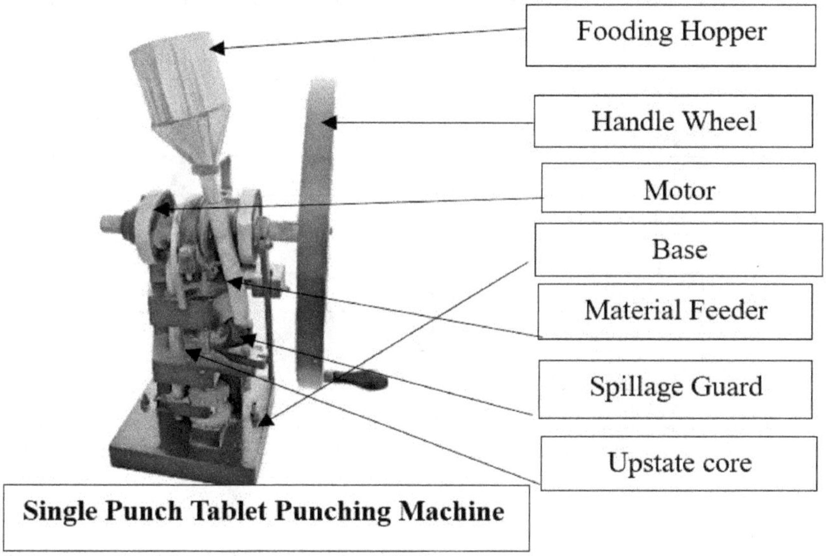

Fig. 2.1 Tablet punching machine.

Packing:

Compressed tablets can be packed in a wide mouth, light resistant containers and should be cover with tight clean cap.

Storage: Store in a well closed container at dry and cool place.

Label the Use: *Analgesic* (Reduces pain) and *Antipyretic* (lower the elevated body temperature).

Labelling:

Ingredient list		Mfg Lic No.
	Formulation name	Mfg date
	(Quantity)	Batch no.
Use	Analgesic & Antipyretic	Exp. Date
Dose	External/Internal Use only	
Storage		Name of manufacturer
Imp. Instruction		

Observation and Evaluation of prepared Paracetamol granules

S. No	Test	Specification	Observation
1.	Description	White color granules	
2.	Nature of granules	Smooth	
3.	Odor	Odorless	
4.	Bulk density		
5.	Tapped density		
6.	Angle of repose	<25	
7.	Car's index	5-15	
8.	Hausner's ratio	1.00-1.11	
9.	Weight of each tablet	500 gm	

Result: Paracetamol tablets were prepared and submitted in a closed, neat labeled container.

QUESTIONS

Q.1 What is the role of starch in the preparation of a tablet?

Q.2 Give another name of Paracetamol?

Q.3 Define term antipyretics?

Q.4 What are lubricants?

Q.5 Give some examples of lubricant?

Q.6 Enlist the defect of tablets?

Q.7 What is tablet?

Q.8 What are the advantages of tablets dosage form?

Answers on page.no: 85

CHAPTER 3

EVALUATION OF PARACETAMOL TABLETS

Aim: To evaluate the 500 mg Paracetamol tablets as per I.P

Requirement:

1. **Apparatus required**: Digital electronic balance, Vernier caliper, Friability apparatus, Monsanto hardness tester, Disintegration apparatus, Dissolution apparatus, UV- spectrophotometer.
2. **Chemical required**: Paracetamol tablets, distilled water, sodium phosphate monobasic monohydrate, sodium phosphate dibasic heptahydrate

Theory:

A tablet is defined as the solid unit dosage form of one or more medicaments with or without excipients meant for oral route. They are prepared either by compression method or by molding method. Available in round, oval or biconvex shapes. Other solid dosage forms available in the market such as capsule, powder, dry powder, and sachet. Excipients used in the formulation of tablets are diluent, binders, disintegrating agent, lubricating agent, glidant, anti-adherent to improve bulkiness, disintegration, dissolution rate and bioavailability of the drug. Aim of the evaluation methods is to confirm the quantity and quality of prepared dosage form as per the standard mentioned in Indian Pharmacopoeia.

Various types of tablets are prepared such as

1. Tablet ingested orally (film coated tablets)
2. Tablet for oral cavity (buccal tablets)
3. Tablets used to prepare solution (effervescent tablets)
4. Tablets for another route (vaginal or implants tablets)

Properties of tablets:

1. The tablet must have sufficient strength against shock and abrasion to resist during manufacturing, packaging, and use.
2. Its size and shape should be reasonable for easy administration.
3. The drug should be uniformly distributed throughout the tablets.
4. Must retain their functional stability and efficacy during storage.
5. The tablet should have the characteristics color and shape for easy identification.
6. They should be accurate and uniform in weight.
7. It should not be too hard to affect the disintegration process in the stomach.
8. It should be chemically and physically stable during storage.
9. It should be attractive.

Active pharmaceutical ingredient (Paracetamol):

Paracetamol is a NASIDs, commonly used to treat fever and mild to moderate pain. Paracetamol is categorized in class 1 (highly soluble and highly permeable), off white in colour with chemical formula $C_8H_9NO_2$, and amorphous in nature. IUPAC name is acetaminophen or para-hydroxy acetanilide. The antipyretic property of Paracetamol is mediated by inhibiting prostaglandin release in the central nervous system and analgesic activity by inhibiting the activity of neurotransmitter N-methyl-D-aspartate (NMDA) to stop nitric oxide pathway.

Standards (IP): Paracetamol tablets contain not less than 95.0% and not more than 105.0% of the stated amount of Paracetamol, $C_8 H_9 NO_2$

Methods used for evaluation of tablets/coated tablets are as follows:

1. Appearance
2. Dimension test
3. Hardness test
4. Friability test
5. Content uniformity test
6. Disintegration test
7. Dissolution test
8. Weight uniformity test

PROCEDURE FOR EVALUATION OF TABLETS

1. **Appearance**: The tablets are observed under a biconvex lens for surface, colour, shape determination.
2. **Dimensions:** The thickness and diameter of a tablets are measured by using Vernier caliper or screw gauge. These values are used to adjust the initial stages of compression.

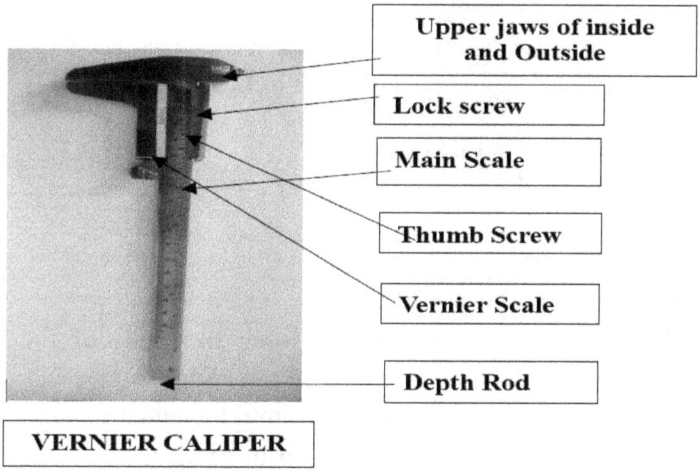

Fig 3.1 Vernier Caliper.

Procedure:

1. Calculate the least count of Vernier Caliper by dividing smallest division on main scale by total number of divisions on Vernier scale.
2. Place one tablet between measuring jaws and record main scale and Vernier scale reading.
3. Measure the thickness of randomly select ten tablets.
4. Take the reading three times and calculate the average thickness of tablets.

3. **Hardness test:** It is defined as the force required to break tablet in a compression test and was measured by using Monsanto hardness test apparatus. This measurement helps in determining the tablets resistance to stress, consistent quality and performance during shipping, manufacture, and packaging. The hardness of uncoated tablet should be more than 4 kg/cm^2. The force is measured in kg/cm^2.

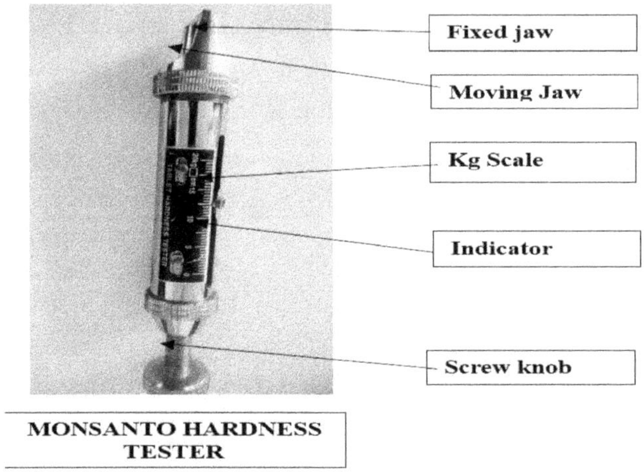

Fig 3.2 Monsanto hardness tester.

Procedure:

1. Place one tablet vertically between the jaws of the Monsanto hardness tester.
2. Rotate the top screw of the tester until the tablet breaks.
3. Record the reading of tablets in terms of kg/cm^2.
4. Adjust the scale to zero for repetition of procedure.
5. Repeat the procedure for 5 tablets.

4. Weight variation test (Uniformity of weight): Weight variation test is performed to ensure the uniformity of drug content in the finished pharmaceutical product. It determines the weight difference from the defined ranges given in the official pharmacopoeias.

Randomly select 20 tablets and weigh them individually. Calculate the average weight and compare it with the individual weight of tablets. Not more than two individuals tablet weight is deviated from the percentage shown in the following table:

Table 3.1 Percentage of deviation allowed as per IP.

S. No	Average weight of tablets	% Deviation
1.	80 mg or less	10
2.	More than 80 mg but less than 250 mg	7.5
3.	250 mg or more	5

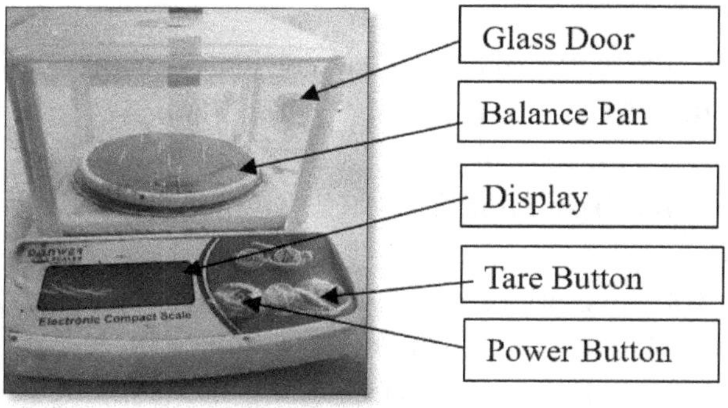

Weight Balance Apparatus

Fig. 3.3 Weight variation test for tablets.

Procedure:

1. Take 20 tablets of 500 mg Paracetamol.
2. Weigh individually the Paracetamol tablets.
3. Again, take weight of same 20 tablets collectively.
4. From collective weight, determine average weight per tablet.
5. Calculate 5% variation of tablets from average value.
6. Compare weights of individual tablet to determine whether they are within permissible limits or not.

5. **Friability test:** Friability test is performed to evaluate ability of tablet to stand wear and tear during packaging, handling and transportation. The friability test apparatus is known as Roche friabilator.

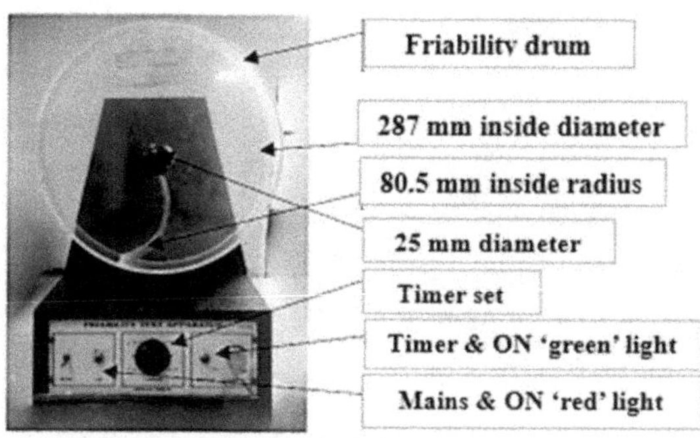

SINGLE DRUM FRIABILATOR

Fig. 3.4 Friabilator apparatus.

Procedure:

1. Take 20 Paracetamol tablets and calculate weight of tablets.
2. Place the 20 tablets in friabilator drum and fix it with the help of knob.
3. Operate the friabilator for 100 revolutions or 25 revolutions in 4 mins.
4. After 100 revolutions, took out the tablets from drum, re-weight tablets and calculate percentage loss in weight.
5. Check tablets for capping, lamination, and chipping.
6. Take another 20 Paracetamol tablets, repeat the previous procedure for friability testing.
7. Calculate the percent friability.

   Weight loss of tablet is the measure of friability and is expressed in percentage as:

$$\%\text{ friability} = \frac{(\text{Initial weight} - \text{final weight})}{(\text{Initial weight})} \times 100$$

6. **Assay of Paracetamol**: Weigh and powder 20 paracetamol tablets. Take a quantity of powder equivalent to 0.15g of paracetamol, to this add 50ml of 0.1M sodium hydroxide, and dilute with 100mL of distilled water, shake it for 15 mins and add sufficient distilled water to make 200mL of solution. Take 10 mL of resulting solution and dilute it to 100 mL with distilled water. To 10mL of this diluted solution, add 10mL of 0.1M sodium hydroxide and again dilute it with 100ml with distilled water. Take absorbance of the final solution at 257 nm by using UV-visible spectrophotometer.

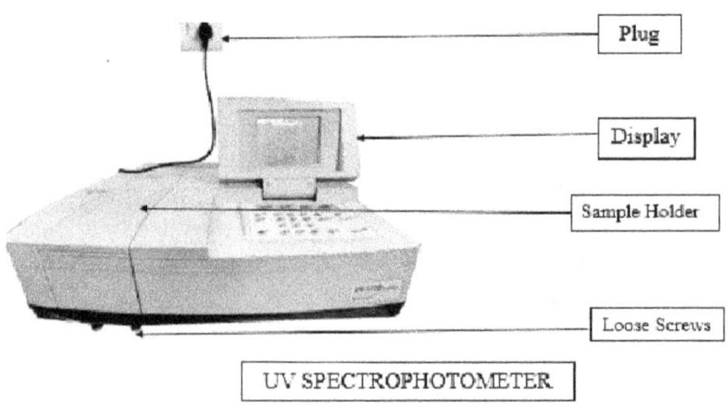

Fig. 3.5 Double beam UV – spectrophotometer.

7. **Disintegration test**: Place one tablet in each of tube of disintegrating apparatus. Suspend the disintegrating tubes in the beaker containing 900ml of distilled water. The basket raises and lowers in the medium with the help of motor for 15 minutes, at the frequency of 29-32 cycles/min and temperature should be maintained at 37±2°C.

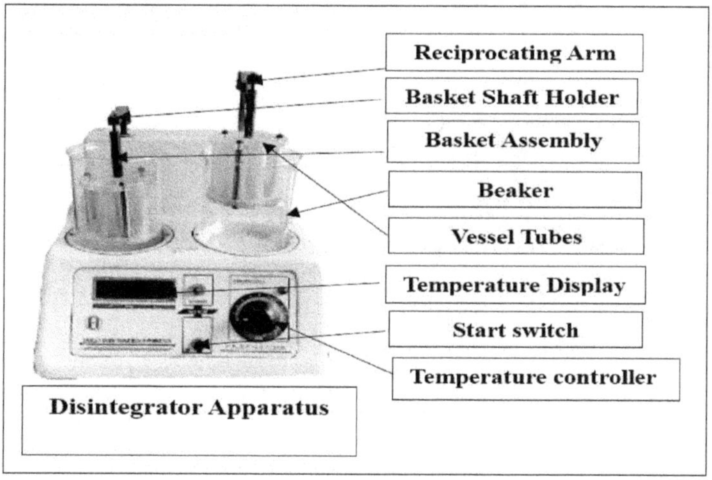

Fig. 3.6 Disintegration test apparatus.

Procedure:

1. Remove basket assembly from the apparatus.
2. Place required quantity of distilled water (800 to 900 ml) into beaker provided with apparatus.
3. Place beaker on its position and switch on the temperature knob to attain temperature of medium to 37°C.
4. Add one tablet in each tube of basket assembly and put discs if necessary.
5. Suspend assembly in liquid medium and operate equipment for 15 minutes.
6. Observe continuously each tablet till disintegration. Record disintegration time for all tablets.
7. At the end of 15 minutes remove basket assembly and observe each tube for any residue of tablet.

8. **Dissolution study:** Dissolution test is used to measure the rate and extent of solution formation from a dosage form.

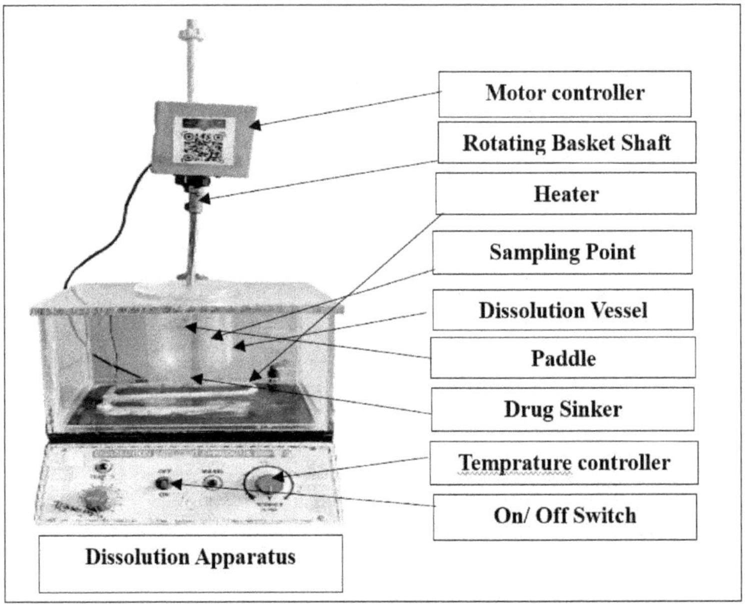

Fig. 3.7 Dissolution Apparatus.

Preparation of dissolution medium:

Phosphate buffer (pH 5.8): Take 900 mL of distilled water in a suitable beaker. Add 20.214 g of Sodium Phosphate Dibasic Heptahydrate and 3.394 g of Sodium Phosphate Monobasic Monohydrate to the solution. Final volume makeup is done by adding distilled water upto the volume of 1 L.

Dissolution apparatus: The dissolution test of paracetamol drug is carried out using **Type-I Paddle dissolution apparatus** (IP). To the 1000mL dissolution beaker, add 900mL of phosphate buffer (pH 5.8) and operate at 50 rpm with a temperature maintained at 37±1°C (throughout the test). Samples is withdrawn at time intervals of 5, 10, 20 and 30minutes and replaced by fresh equal volume of dissolution medium, the withdrawn sample is filter and assay at 243 nm by using UV-visible spectroscopy. Phosphate buffer used as blank.

Procedure:

1. Use Type- I dissolution apparatus, as per IP, for the dissolution test.
2. Immerse one paracetamol tablet in 900 mL of dissolution medium (Phosphate buffer pH 5.8).
3. Maintain the temperature of dissolution medium 37 ± 0.2°C.

4. Rotate the basket at a speed of 50 rpm and in the interval of every 10, 5mL sample is withdrawn with the help of pipette and replace with fresh medium of phosphate buffer (pH 5.8).
5. Record the absorbance of the sample solutions at λ=243 nm (wavelength= λ) using the phosphate buffer as a blank.
6. Plot a graph (calibration curve) between concentration of drug on x-axis vs absorbance on y-axis.
7. Calculate concentration of drug, amount of drug release, percentage of drug release using followed formulas:

1. Concentration of drug released is calculated by:

$$Y = mX + C$$

Where, Y is absorbance, m is slope, C is intercept, X is concentration (mcg/ml)

2. Amount of drug released is calculated by:

Amount of drug released (mg)=

[Concentration X Dilution Factor X Volume of Dissolution medium] / 1000

3. Percentage of drug release is calculated by:

% Drug release = Amt of drug released (mg) X 100 / Dose (mg)

Observation and evaluation:

1. Appearance:

Test	Observation	Inference
Colour	Uniform/non-uniform	
Depression	Absent/present	
Polish	Uniform/non-uniform	
Surface roughness	Smooth/irregular	
Cracks	Absent/present	

2. Dimension:

No. of Tablets	**1**	**2**	**3**	**4**	**5**	**6**	**7**	**8**	**9**	**10**
Diameter in mm										
Thickness in mmm										

Result: The diameter of tablet was found to be -------- and thickness of tablet was found to be -------.

3. Table hardness:

No. of tablets	1	2	3	4	5
Hardness in Kg/cm^2					

Result: The tablets pass/fail the hardness test

4. Weight variation:

No. of tablet	1	2	3	4	5	6	7	8	9	10
Weight (gm)										
Pass/Fail										
No. of tablet	11	12	13	14	15	16	17	18	19	20
Weight(gm)										
Pass/Fail										

1. Average weight = Collective weight of 20 tablets/ 20
2. 5 % deviation from average weight
   Percentage deviation = 5 x average weight of tablet/100
3. Upper limit Upper limit = Average weight per tablet + 5 % deviation from average
4. Lower limit Lower limit = Average weight per tablet + 5 % deviation from average.

Average weight per tablet	
5 % deviation from average	
Upper limit	
Lower limit	

Result: Average weight per tablet was found to be--------- mg. 5 % deviation from average was -------- mg. The weights of individual tablets were lies within permissible limits or not.

5. Friability

1. Weight of 20 tablets before friability test (w_0) _____ gm
2. Weight of 20 tablets after friability test (w_1) _____ gm

% friability = (Initial weight W_0-final weightW_1)/ (Initial weightW_0) x 100

Result: Friability of given Paracetamol tablet is found to be _______ %

6. Disintegration Test (DT):

Tablet No.	1	2	3	4	5	6	Average DT
Disintegration time (min)							
Residue on screen (yes/no)							

Result: Disintegration time of given paracetamol tablet was found to be _______ min. No residue found on screen of basket assembly at the end test.

7. Dissolution Test:

Calculation of percentage drug release

S. No	Time	Absorbance	Concentration	Amount of drug release	% of drug release
1.					
2					
3					
4.					
5.					
6.					
7.					
8.					

Result: Dissolution studies of paracetamol tablets were performed, and the percentage of drug release was found to be

Result: The tablets *pass or fail* the evaluation test as per IP

QUESTIONS

Q.1 Define Tablet?
Q.2 What are the ideal properties of tablet?
Q.3 Define tablet hardness?
Q.4 What is Glidants?
Q.5 What is compressed tablet?
Q.6 What is a friability test?
Q.7 What is a dissolution test?
Q.8 Write down the working of Pfizer tablet hardness tester?
Q.9 Write note on disintegration test?
Q.10 What is uniformity weight?

Answers on page.no: 85

CHAPTER 4

PREPARATION AND EVALUATION OF ASPIRIN TABLETS

Aim: To prepare, evaluate and submit 50 Aspirin tablets each containing 300 mg of aspirin, by wet granulation method (IP).

Apparatus requirements:

1. **Apparatus required:** Mortar and pestle, graduated measuring cylinder 100ml, beaker, sieve no.#10, #22, #44, #60, hot air oven, dryer, compression machine.
2. **Chemicals required:** Aspirin, lactose, methylcellulose, alcohol, and PEG 4000.

Theory:

A tablet is a solid unit dosage form intended for oral administration that contains one or more medications, with or without excipients. Aspirin (acetylsalicylic acid) is a non-steroidal anti- inflammatory drug, belongs to class 1 (highly soluble and highly permeable) of the Biopharmaceutical Classification System (BCS) and used as antipyretic, anti-inflammatory and antiplatelet used to reduce fever and mild to moderate headaches. It is recommended in people who have a history of cardiovascular disease such as heart attack or angina. Physicians advice to take aspirin in low doses as "blood thinner" to prevent blood clots. Aspirin as tablet is available in extended-release form, normal tablet, and delayed release form. In the preparation of aspirin tablets, Aspirin is used as API ingredient, polyvinyl pyrrolidone as binder, starch as disintegrating agent, talc as glidant and magnesium stearate as lubricant. Due to hygroscopic nature, granules of aspirin are prepared using a non-aqueous binder, such as PVP in alcohol.

Tablet additives are compounds that are used in addition to active substances and inert in nature. Among them are:

1. **Diluents** are fillers used to give tablets the necessary weight. For example, lactose, microcrystalline cellulose, and inorganic dicalcium salts.
2. **Binding agents** used to create cohesive mass for direct compression. For example, cellulose derivatives, tragacanth mucilage, glucose syrup, and gelatin solution.
3. **Disintegrating agents** are substances that are added to tablets to help them to break when they come in contact with digestive juices. For example, alginates, clays, cellulose, cellulose derivatives, and dry starch
4. **Anti-frictional agents:** enhancing the powder particle flow properties For example, corn starch, talc.
5. **Lubricants** are used to stop tablets from sticking to dies and punches. For example: Stearic acid, magnesium stearate, calcium stearate, paraffin, talc, and PEG 400, 600, 8000.
6. **Glidants** assist in granules moving freely from the hopper into the die cavity and reduce the resistance between the particles. For example, talc, maize starch.

Compressed tablets are prepared by three methods:

1. Wet granulation method
2. Dry granulation method
3. Direct granulation method

In the pharmaceutical industry, wet granulation is a frequently employed technique for manufacturing tablets, capsules, and other solid dosage forms. This method helps in improving the flowability and uniformity of powder.

Following Steps involved in wet granulation method are:

(a) Weighing and blending of ingredients in geometrical order
(b) Preparation of damp mass by adding binding agents.
(c) Converting the damp mass into wet granules with the help of sieve
(d) Drying of granules
(e) Sieving to obtain uniform granule size
(f) Addition of lubricant
(g) Compressed into tablet form by compression machine.

PREPARATION OF ASPIRIN TABLETS:

Table 4.1 Aspirin tablets formulation table.

S. No	Ingredients for	1 tablet(mg)	For 40 tablets(g)
1.	Aspirin (drug)	300mg	
2.	Polyvinyl pyrrolidone	q. s.	
3.	Talc	10 mg	
4.	Magnesium stearate	10mg	
5.	Starch	15mg	

q. s = quantity sufficient

A. Preparation of granules:

1. Weigh prescribed quantity of disintegrating (starch) and lubricating (magnesium stearate, Talc) agents, pass through sieve no. 60# and divide into two equal parts, first part will be added during wet granulation and second part add after in-dried granules.
2. For wet granulation, weigh the required quantity of aspirin and pass through sieve no. 60#, blend together with first part of lubricating and disintegrating agent as mention in step 1 and mix them in a pestle mortar using glass rod.
3. Prepare 10% PVP solution in ethanol. Add drop by drop solution of 10% PVP to the pestle mortar and form a wet mass.
4. The wet mass is forced to pass through a sieve no. 60# or 80#.
5. Dry the wet granules at 60° C for 1 hour by spreading granules on the tray of oven.
6. Dried granules are passed through a sieve no. 16 # or 10 # and mixed with second part of the disintegrating agent and lubricating agent.
7. Compress the granules to prepare the tablet.
8. Prepared tablets are stored properly for further evaluation.

B. Punching of Tablet:

1. Weigh the granules equivalent to 300mg of Aspirin (i.e. about 1.34 g of granules)
2. Set the table punching machine.
3. Fill weighed granules into the die cavity.
4. Apply optimum pressure on upper punch to compress the granules.

5. After compression, eject prepared tablets and check for desired hardness with hardness tester.
6. If the tablet has sufficient hardness, then repeat the procedure to prepare the next tablet.

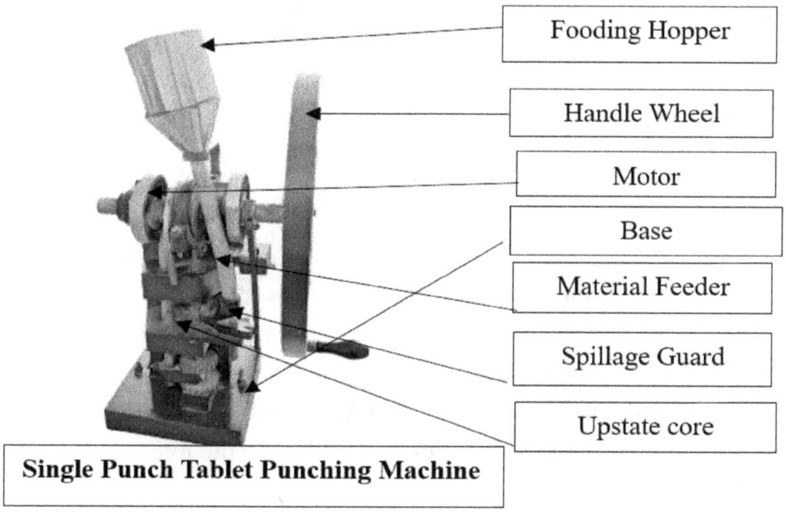

Fig.4.1 Tablet punching machine.

Packing:

Compressed tablets can be packed in a wide mouth, light resistant containers and should be cover with tight clean cap.

Storage: Store in a well close container in a dry and cool place.

Label the Use: *Analgesic* (Reduces pain) and *Antipyretic* (lower the elevated body temperature).

Labelling:

Ingredient list		**Mfg Lic No.**
	Formulation name	**Mfg date**
	(Quantity)	**Batch no.**
Use	**Analgesic & Antipyretic**	**Exp. Date**
	External/Internal Use only	
Storage		**Name of manufacturer**
Imp. Instruction		

Evaluation methods for Aspirin tablets:

1. **Appearance**: The tablets are observe under a biconvex lens for surface, colour, shape determination. The surface of tablet should be smooth and crack free.
2. **Tablet dimensions:** The thickness and diameter of a tablet are measure by using Vernier caliper or screw gauge (Refer Fig. 3.1 of Experiment 03). These values are used to check the dimension of tablet as per standard monograph and help in adjustment of initial stages of compression.

   Procedure:

   1. Calculate the least count of Vernier Caliper by dividing smallest division on main scale by total number of divisions on Vernier scale.
   2. Place one tablet between measuring jaws and record main scale and Vernier scale reading.
   3. Measure the thickness for randomly select 10 tablets.
   4. Take the reading three times and calculate the average thickness of tablet.
3. **Hardness test:** Tablet hardness is measured by using Monsanto hardness test apparatus (Refer Fig. 3.2 of Experiment 03).

   Procedure:

   1. Place the tablet between the jaws of the Monsanto hardness tester.
   2. Rotate the top screw of the tester until the tablet breaks.
   3. Record the reading of tablets in terms of $kg/cm^{2.}$
   4. Adjust the scale to zero for repetition of procedure.
   5. Again, rotate top screw of the tester to create pressure on tablet.
   6. Continue the rotation of screw till tablets breaks.
   7. At this stage, record the reading in terms of kg/cm^2.
   8. Repeat the procedure for the next tablet.
4. **Weight variation test:** Weigh 20 tablets individually with the help of weighting balance machine shown in Fig. 3.3 of Experiment 03. Calculate the average weight. Compare individual weight of tablet with the average weight. Not more than two individual weights of tablet should be deviated from the percentage shown in the following table:

Table 4.2 Table for weight variation test.

S. No	Average weight of tablets	Percentage Deviation
1.	80 mg or less	10
2.	More than 80 mg but less than 250 mg	7.5
3.	250 mg or more	5

Procedure:

1. Randomly select 20 aspirin tablets
2. Weigh individually all Aspirin tablets taken and record the weight in observation table.
3. Again, take weight of same 20 tablets collectively.
4. From collective weight, calculate average weight per tablet.
5. If weight of individual tablet is more than 250 mg (as per Table 4.2), consider 5% variation.
7. Calculate upper limit and lower limit.
8. Compare weights of individual tablet to determine whether they are within permissible limits or not.

5. **Friability test:** Friability is a measure of mechanical strength of the tablet. If a tablet shows more friability, it may not remain intact during packaging, transport, or handling. Roche friabilator is used to determine the friability using following procedure, shown in Fig. 3.4 of Experiment 03.

Procedure:

1. Take 20 Aspirin tablets and calculate weight of 20 tablets.
2. Place the 20 tablets in friabilator drum and fix it with the help of knob.
3. Operate the friabilator for 100 revolutions or 25 revolutions in 4 mins.
4. After 100 revolutions, took out the tablets from drum, re-weight tablets and calculate percentage loss in weight.
5. Check tablets for capping, lamination, and chipping.
6. Take another 20 Aspirin tablets, repeat the previous procedure for friability testing.
7. Calculate the percent friability.

   Weight loss of tablet is the measure of friability and is expressed in percentage as: % friability = (Initial weight-final weight)/ Initial weight) x 100

6. **Assay of Aspirin:** Take randomly 20 Aspirin tablets and powder them using pestle mortar. Weigh a quantity of the powder containing amount equivalent to 100 mg of Aspirin/ API and transferred to a 50 mL volumetric flask add 30ml of 0.5 M sodium hydroxide, boil gently for 10 mins, cool and titrate the with 0.5 M HCl using phenol red solution as indicator. Repeat the procedure for blank (without drug). The difference between the titrations represents the amount of sodium hydroxide required.

   1ml of 0.5M sodium hydroxide is equivalent to 0.04504g of Aspirin

7. **Disintegration test**: Place one tablet in each of tube of disintegrating apparatus. Suspend the disintegrating tubes in the beaker containing 900mL of distilled water. The basket raises and lowers in the medium with the help of motor for 15 minutes, at the frequency of 29-32 cycles/min and at temperature should be maintained at 37±2°C.

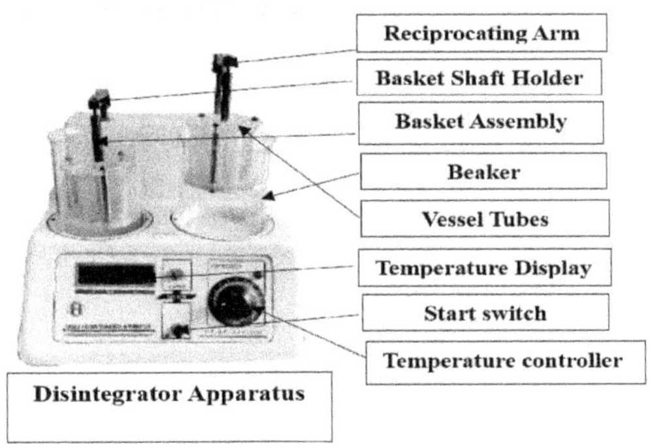

Fig 4.2 Disintegration test apparatus.

Procedure:

1. Remove basket assembly from the apparatus.
2. Place required quantity of distilled water (800 to 900 ml) into beaker provided with apparatus.
3. Place beaker on its position and switch on the temperature knob to attain temperature of medium to 37±2°C.
4. Add one tablet in each tube of basket assembly and put discs if necessary.
5. Suspend assembly in liquid medium and operate equipment for 15 minutes.

6. Observe continuously each tablet till disintegration. Record disintegration time for all tablets.
7. At the end of 15 minutes remove basket assembly and observe each tube for any residue of tablet.

8. **Dissolution study:** Dissolution test is used to measure the rate and extent of solution formation from a dosage form.

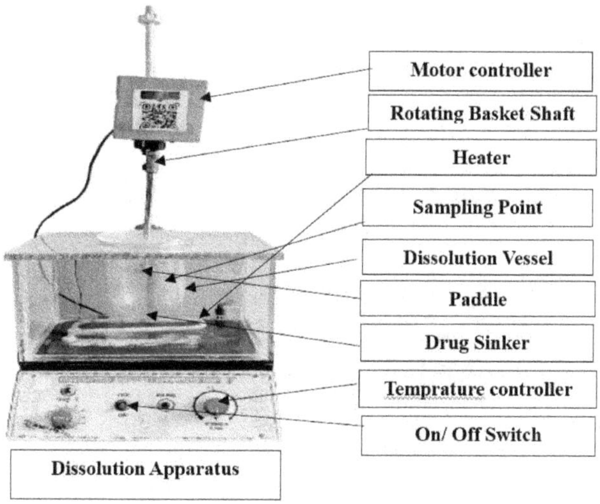

Fig 4.3 Dissolution Apparatus.

Preparation of dissolution medium:

Buffer solution (pH 4.5): 500mL of buffer solution (pH 4.5), is prepared by dissolving 2.99g sodium acetate and 1.66mL of glacial acetic acid with sufficient water and dilute to 1000mL with distilled water.

Dissolution apparatus: The dissolution test of Aspirin drug is carried out using **Type-II Basket dissolution apparatus (IP)**. To the 1000mL dissolution beaker, add 900mL of sodium acetate (pH 4.5) and operate at 50 rpm with a temperature maintained at 37±1°C (throughout the test) for 45 min. Samples is withdrawn at time intervals of 5, 10, 20, 30 and 45mins and replaced by fresh equal volume of dissolution medium, the withdrawn sample is filter and assay at 243 nm by using UV-visible spectroscopy. Sodium acetate (pH4.5) used as blank.

Procedure:

1. Use Type- II dissolution apparatus, as per IP, for the dissolution test.
2. Immerse one Aspirin tablet in 900 mL of dissolution medium.

3. The temperature of the dissolution medium is maintained at 37 ± 0.2°C.
4. The basket is rotate at a speed of 50 rpm and in the interval of every 10min,5mL sample is withdrawn with the help of pipette and replace with fresh medium of sodium acetate (pH 4.5).
5. Record the absorbance of the sample solutions at λ=265 nm (wavelength= λ) using the sodium acetate as a blank.
6. Plot a graph (calibration curve) between concentration of drug on x-axis vs absorbance on y-axis.
7. Calculate concentration of drug, amount of drug release, percentage of drug release using followed formulas:

(i) Concentration of drug released is calculated by:

$$Y = mX + C$$

Where, Y is absorbance, m is slope, C is intercept, X is concentration (mcg/ml)

(ii) Amount of drug released is calculated by:

Amount of drug released (mg)= [Concentration X Dilution Factor X Volume of Dissolution medium] / 1000

(iii) Percentage of drug release is calculated by:

% Drug release = Amt of drug released (mg) X 100 / Dose (mg)

Observation and evaluation:

1. Appearance:

Test	Observation	Inference
Colur	Uniform/non-uniform	
Depression	Absent/present	
Polish	Uniform/non-uniform	
Surface roughness	Smooth/irregular	
Cracks	Absent/present	

2. Dimension:

No.of Tablets	1	2	3	4	5	6	7	8	9	10
Diameter in mm										
Thickness in mmm										

Result: The diameter of tablet was found to be -------- and thickness of tablet was found to be -------.

3. Tablet hardness:

No. of tablets	1	2	3	4	5
Hardness in Kg/cm^2					

Result: The tablets pass/fail the hardness test

4. Weight variation:

No. of tablet		1	2	3	4	5	6	7	8	9	10
Weight (gm)											
Pass/Fail											
No. of tablet		11	12	13	14	15	16	17	18	19	20
Weight(gm)											
Pass/Fail											

- Average weight = Collective weight of 20 tablets/ 20
- 5 % deviation from average weight
- Percent deviation = 5 x average weight of tablet/100
- Upper limit Upper limit = Average weight per tablet + 5 % deviation from average
- Lower limit Lower limit = Average weight per tablet + 5 % deviation from average.

Average weight per tablet	
5 % deviation from average	
Upper limit	
Lower limit	

Result: Average weight per tablet was found to be ------ 5 percentage deviation from average is ------. The weights of individual tablets are lies within permissible limits------or not

5. Friability:

1. Weight of 20 tablets before friability test (w_o)_____ gm
2. Weight of 20 tablets after friability test (w_1) _____ gm

   % friability = (Initial weight W_0-final weight W_1)/ Initial weight W_0) x 100

   Result: Friability of given aspirin tablet was found to be _______ %

6. Disintegration Test (DT):

Tablet No.	1	2	3	4	5	6	Average DT
Disintegration time (min)							
Residue on screen(yes/no)							

Disintegration time of given aspirin tablet is found to be _____.
No residue found on screen of basket assembly at the end of test.

7. Dissolution Test:

S. No	Time	Absorbance	Concentration	Amt. of drug release	% of drug release
1.					
2.					
3.					
4.					
5.					
6.					
7.					
8.					

Result: Dissolution studies of aspirin tablets were performed, and the percentage of drug release was found to be

Result: The tablets *pass or fail* the evaluation test as per I.P

QUESTIONS

Q.1 Describe hypodermic tablets?

Q.2 Discuss features of Tablets.

Q.3 What is crystal bridging during wet granulation?

Q.4 What are the steps involved in Direct compression?

Q.5 Why dry granulation method is used?

Q.6 Write the name of Pharmacopoeia or official tests for tablets?

Q.7 Discuss about the advantages of wet granulation?

Answers on page.no: 86

CHAPTER 5

FILM COATING OF TABLETS /GRANULES

Aim: To perform film coating of Tablets

Requirements:

1. **Apparatus Required:** Beaker, measuring cylinder, stirrer, coating pan, spray gun.
2. **Chemical Required:** Hydroxy propyl methylcellulose, PEG 400, iron oxide yellow, titanium dioxide, purified water.

Theory:

An active pharmaceutical ingredient (API) is the biologically active part of a pharmaceutical product (tablet, pill, cream, or injection) that has the required effect on the body to treat a condition. APIs have their own unique physio-chemical characteristics. Some of the characteristics that make drugs challenging to manufacture in solid dosage form include their hygroscopic nature, disagreeable odor, harsh taste, and sensitivity to light. Film coating and sugar coating are two methods used for tablet coating in order to overcome following challenges. Film coating involves the deposition of a thin layer of film-forming polymeric material on the tablet core. The process was introduced in 1950s by Dr. Dale Wurster, a professor at the university of Wisconsin as an improvement on the traditional sugar-coating process. Tablet film coating is performed in two ways: 1) aqueous film coating (water is used as a solvent); and 2) non-aqueous film coating (organic solvents are used). A non-aqueous solvent-based coating can be used for drugs that hydrolyze easily in the presence of water. Film coating helps in improving the shelf life by providing a protective barrier between the drug and the surrounding environment, making dosage form easier to swallow. It is also used to delay the delivery and uptake of medications until the medication passes through the stomach. The main components of film-coating formulations are: Polymer (HPMC, ethyl cellulose, shellac), Plasticizer (PEG 400, propylene glycol), Colourants / Opacifiers (titanium dioxide, iron oxide yellow), Solvent / Vehicle (purified water, ethanol).

Advantage of Film coating includes:

1. Help in making the taste, odor, or color of the drug.
2. Provide physical and chemical protection to the drug from external environment.
3. Protect the drug from the gastric environment of stomach.
4. Improve the pharmaceutical elegance.
5. Significant reduction in processing time.
6. Moderating the release profile of the drug substance.

PREPARATION OF FILM COATING

Table 5.1 Film coating formulation table.

S. No	Ingredients	Quantity given %w/w	Quantity taken
1.	Polyethylene glycol (PEG) 400	0.8g	
2.	Hydroxy propyl methylcellulose	7.5g	
3.	Iron oxide yellow	0.6g	
4.	Titanium dioxide	3.1g	
5.	Purified water	88.0ml	

Procedure:

Prepare uncoated tablets by wet granulation method, then perform coating of uncoated tablet with the help of film coating solution in following steps:

A. Preparation of Coating Solution:

1. Weigh prescribed quantity of PEG (table 5.1), to prepare coating solution by dissolving in one-third of purified water with continuous stirring.

2. Add slowly the prescribed quantity of HPMC, titanium dioxide and iron oxide yellow by continuous stirring.
3. Add the remaining part of purified water to the above solution with constant stirring for 15-20 min.
4. Filter the prepare coating solution by using filter paper.

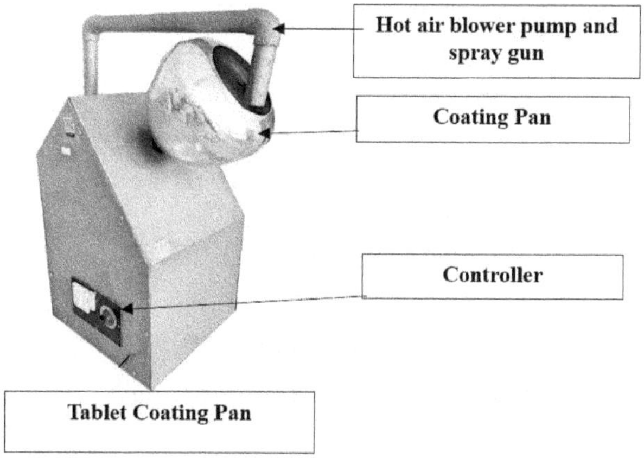

Fig 5.1 Coating Pan.

B. Coating of tablets by prepared solution:

1. Preheat the coating pan to 40°C- 50°C with the hot air.
2. Place uncoated tablets in the coating pan.
3. Adjust the air pressure and spraying speed of the spray gun.
4. Turn on the coating pan and change the rotation speed to 20 rpm.
5. Spray the coating liquid onto the uncoated tablets until a uniform film coating is formed.
6. Stop spraying and keep the coating pan running for a few more minutes to avoid sticking of coated tablets.
7. Allow coated tablets to dry in pan for 5 to 10 min by blowing hot air.

Packing: Store in a suitable well closed container.

Storage: Store below 25°C and keep away from children and sunlight.

Observations of film coated tablets:

S. No	Test	Specification	Observation
1.	Coating	uniform/ non-uniform	
2.	Surface	smooth/ rough	
3.	Glossy	absent/ present	
4.	Cracks	Absent/ present	

Results: Film coating of tablets was performed uniformly.

QUESTIONS

Q.1 What are the methods used for tablet coating?

Q.2 What are the problems associate with sugar coating?

Q.3 Write the names of polymers used in film coating?

Q.4 What is Plasticizer and give examples?

Q.5 What are the steps involved in sugar coating?

Q.6 Name colorants used in Film Coating?

Q.7 What is film coating?

Q.8 Enlist the defects found in film coating?

Q.9 What is the role of solvent in film coating?

Q.10 What is Orange -Peel effect in coating?

Answers on page.no: 87

CHAPTER 6

FORMULATION OF ENTERIC COATED TABLETS OF OMEPRAZOLE

Aim: To prepare and evaluate 10 tablets of enteric coated omeprazole.

Requirements:

1. **Apparatus required:** Mortar and pestle, beaker, sieve, glass rod, pH meter, conventional coating pan with one spray gun, air compressor
2. **Chemical required:** Omeprazole, lactose hydrate, maize starch, sodium lauryl sulphate, light magnesium oxide, hydroxyl propyl methyl cellulose (HPMC), magnesium stearate, purified water, cellulose powder, propylene glycol, absolute alcohol, methacrylic acid copolymer, phosphate buffer, fumed silica.

Theory:

Pharmaceutical drugs in a solid form meant for oral administration are known as oral solid dosage forms. Lozenges, tablets, capsules, powders, and granules are among them. These dosage forms are generally easy to produce, handle, and distribute. Since they are readily absorbed and can be taken with or without meals, hence convenient for patients to consume. Several factors, including the drug's therapeutic activity, stability, and patient preference, influence the choice of solid dosage form.

Enteric coating is one of the methods used to overcome some of the weakness of oral dosage form like gastrointestinal irritation, degradation in acidic pH etc. Enteric coating is the process in which layer of polymers are applied over core tablets to prevent them from dissolving in acidic pH of stomach. Polymers used for enteric coating are shellac, polyvinyl acetate phthalate (PVAP), cellulose acetate phthalate (CAP), hydroxypropyl methylcellulose (HPMC) etc. Enteric coating involves three steps:

1. Core tablet formulation
2. Seal coating of core tablet
3. Enteric coating of sealed tablet

Core tablets are compressed-coated tablet consists of two parts; *one is an internal drug core,* and *another is an outside coating shell.* The outer layer surrounds the inner core and controls the release of the drug. Seal coating is performed to prevent core tablet from moisture and interaction of drug with acidic enteric coating. For seal coating, HPMC solution is prepared in phosphate buffer. For enteric coating, HPMC phthalate polymer is used in acetone, isopropyl alcohol, which prevent tablet degradation in acidic environment of stomach.

Advantage of Enteric coating:

1. Maintain the stability of active pharmaceutical ingredient in acidic environment of Stomach e.g. Omeprazole.
2. Help in reducing the side effects of drug such as nausea, gastric irritation, bleeding.
3. Help in making the bitter taste of drug.
4. Provide sustained/ controlled release of drug.

Active pharmaceutical ingredient (Omeprazole):

Omeprazole is a proton pump inhibitor and used to treat several conditions such as peptic ulcer, heart burn, gastrointestinal reflux disease, gastric ulcer. It shows powerful inhibitory action against secretion of gastric juice. Due to degradation nature of Omeprazole in acidic pH, it is formulated in enteric coated dosage form. Omeprazole is categorized into class II of BCS classification.

PREPARATION OF ENTERIC COATING TABLETS OF OMEPRAZOLE:

Table 6.1 Enteric coated Omeprazole tablets formulation table.

S. No	Ingredients	Quantity given(mg)	Quantity taken
	Core tablet ingredients		
1.	Omeprazole	20mg	
2.	Lactose hydrate	76mg	
3.	Maize starch	60 mg	
4.	Sodium lauryl sulphate	2mg	
5.	Fumed silica	0.6mg	

contd..

6.	Magnesium stearate	1.4mg	
	Sub coating ingredients I		
1.	HPMC	0.25g	
2.	Phosphate buffer (7.4)	q.s	
	Sub-coating ingredients II		
1.	Cellulose powder	0.96g	
2.	Light Magnesium oxide	0.77g	
3.	Magnesium stearate	0.77g	
4.	Absolute alcohol	100mL	
	Enteric coating material		
1.	Propylene glycol	4.2%	
2.	Purified water	q.s	
3.	Methacrylic acid copolymer	70%	

q.s=quantity sufficient

A. Preparation of core tablet:

1. For preparation of core tablets, weigh all the ingredients enlisted in the formulation table (6.1) accurately and sieve through sieve no #60.
2. Put together, the weighed and sieved omeprazole, magnesium stearate, sodium lauryl sulphate and maize starch into the pestle and mortar and triturate for 10 minutes.
3. To the above mixture, add weighed quantity of lactose hydrate and fumed silica, mix for another 5 mins and sieve through sieve no #60.
4. The resulting mixture is ready to compressed in a tablet form by compression machine, as described in previous experiment 02.
5. Prepared tablets should be stored properly for coating.

B. Procedure for sub-coating (I & II) and enteric coating:

1. Sub-coating, I:

Weigh 0.25g of HPMC polymer and dissolve it in phosphate buffer 7.4 to obtain 0.25% w/v solution HPMC. For sub- coating of core tablet, the coating solution is added to the coating pan as per the procedure mentioned in Experiment 5 (Procedure B). Dry the coated tablets.

2. Sub-coating II:

1. Weigh all ingredients of sub-coating II mentioned in table (6.1) and dissolve in 250 ml beaker containing 100ml of absolute alcohol.
2. The above mixture is stirring for 45 mins using homogenizer stirrer for homogenous suspension.

3. The prepared sub-coating II solution add to the coating pan as per the procedure mentioned in Experiment 5 (Procedure B). Dry the coated tablets.

3. Enteric coating of tablet:

1. Weigh all ingredients of Enteric coating as mentioned in table (6.1).
2. Take 250 mL beaker, add 100ml of purified water and propylene glycol and stir it for 10 mins using homogenizer stirrer
3. To the above mixture, add methacrylic copolymer and stir it again for 15 mins.
4. Preheat the coated pan (40°C± 5°C) for 10 mins, then add prepared enteric coating solution to this as per the procedure mentioned in Experiment 5 (Procedure B). Dry the coated tablets.

Packing: Store in aluminum blisters or tight closed container.

Storage: Store in cool and dry place.

Use: To treat peptic ulcer, heart burn, gastrointestinal reflux disease, gastric ulcer.

Labelling

Ingredient list		**Mfg Lic No.**
	Formulation name	**Mfg date**
	(Quantity)	**Batch no.**
Use		**Exp. Date**
	External/Internal Use only	
Storage		**Name of manufacturer**
Instruction		

Evaluation methods for enteric coated Omeprazole tablets:

1. Evaluation of appearance, dimension, hardness, friability and uniformity of weight is performed as per the procedure mentioned in Experiment 03.
2. **Disintegration test**: Place one tablet in each of tube of disintegrating apparatus. Suspend the disintegrating tubes in the beaker containing 900mL of 0.1M HCl. The basket raises and lowers in the medium with the help of motor for 2 hours, at the frequency of 29-32 cycles/min and temperature should be maintained at 37±2°C. If no tablets show the sign of cracks, allow to follow the next step.

Again, replace the medium with phosphate buffer pH 6.8, place same tablets in each of tube of disintegrating apparatus. The basket raises and lowers in the medium with discs with the help of motor for 60 mins, at the frequency of 29-32 cycles/min and temperature should be maintained at 37±2°C. If tablets fail to comply and adhere/stick to the disc, repeat the test on another six tablets the tablets pass the test if all six have disintegrated.

3. **Dissolution test**:

Dissolution medium: 0.1N HCl (pH 1.2) is used for 1st two hours then Phosphate buffer (pH 6.8) is used for remaining hours

Dissolution test: The dissolution test of enteric coated Omeprazole tablets is carried out using **Type-II Paddle dissolution apparatus** (USP) in the dissolution medium of 0.1 N HCl for 2 hours and then the phosphate buffer pH 6.8 for 1 hour. The temperature should be maintained at 37±0.5°C and a constant paddle rotation speed of 100 rpm.

Procedure:

1. Use Type- II dissolution apparatus, as per USP, for the dissolution test.
2. Immerse one tablet in 900 ml of dissolution medium (0.1N HCl, pH 1.2)
3. Maintain the temperature of dissolution medium at 37 ± 0.2°C.
4. Rotate the basket at a speed of 100 rpm and in the interval of every 15 mins, 5ml sample is withdrawn with the help of pipette and replace with fresh dissolution medium.
5. After 2 hours, replace the dissolution medium with fresh phosphate buffer pH 6.8.
6. Maintain the temperature of dissolution medium at 37 ± 0.2°C. Rotate the basket at a speed of 100 rpm and in the interval of every 15 mins, 5ml sample is withdrawn with the help of pipette and replace with fresh dissolution medium.
7. Record the absorbance of the sample solutions at λ=271 nm (wavelength= λ) using the phosphate buffer as a blank.
8. Plot a graph (calibration curve) between concentration of drug on x-axis vs absorbance on y-axis.
9. Calculate concentration of drug, amount of drug release, percentage of drug release using followed formulas:

i) Concentration of drug released is calculated by:

$$Y = mX + C$$

Where, Y is absorbance, m is slope, C is intercept, X is concentration (mcg/ml)

ii) Amount of drug released is calculated by:

Amount of drug released (mg)= [Concentration X Dilution Factor X Volume of Dissolution medium] / 1000

iii) Percentage of drug release is calculated by:

% Drug release = Amt of drug released (mg) X 100 / Dose (mg)

Observations of enteric coated tablets

S. No	Test	Specification	Observation
1.	Coating	uniform/ non-uniform	
2.	Surface	smooth/ rough	
3.	Glossy	absent/ present	
4.	Cracks	Absent/ present	

Evaluation table of enteric coated tablets

S. No	Sample	weight variation (mg)	Hardness (kg/cm²)	Friability (%)	Disintegration time (Sec/min)	%Drug Content Release
1.						
2.						
3.						

Evaluation of dissolution profile of enteric coated tablets

S. No	Sample	%Drug content Release	%Drug content Release	%Drug content Release	%Drug content Release	%Drug content Release	%Drug content Release
1							
2							
3							

Results: 10 Omeprazole enteric-coated tablets were prepared and prepared tablets passed *or* fail the evaluation test.

QUESTIONS

Q.1 What is tablet press machine?

Q.2 What are the different types of tablets?

Q.3 What is an enteric-coated tablet?

Q.4 Enlist the polymers used for enteric coating?

Q.5 What is the role of disintegrating agents in tablets?

Q.6 Why coating of tablets is performed?

Q.7 How core tablets are prepared?

Answers on page.no: 88

CHAPTER 7

PREPARATION AND EVALUATION OF TETRACYCLINE CAPSULES

Aim: To Prepare and evaluate 20 capsules of 250 mg Tetracycline hydrochloride.

Requirements:

1. **Apparatus required:** Mortar and pestle, empty gelatin capsules, sieve, hand operated capsule filling machine, volumetric flask, pipette, beaker, stopwatch, measuring cylinder, Whatman filter paper, UV spectrophotometer, disintegration test apparatus.
2. **Chemical Required**: Tetracycline, dried starch powder, dried talcum.

Theory:

Capsules are solid unit dosage forms in which a drug or mixture of drug is enclosed in a hard gelatin capsule or soft gelatin capsule intended for oral administration. The capsule shell is made up of gelatin. Based on the percentage of gelatin and plasticizer, consistency of capsule is soft or hard. Capsules are available in the range of 000 to 5. Number 5 capsule is the smallest capsule shell. Gelatin is obtained by the hydrolysis of collagen obtained from the skin and bones of animals. Nowadays, it is available in the form of a fine powder, a coarse powder, shreds, flakes, or sheets. Gelatin is more soluble in hot water than in cold water; a gelatin capsule rapidly dissolves and exposes its contents in the gastric media of the body.

Tetracycline is a bacteriostatic broad-spectrum antibiotic, active against a wide variety of gram-positive and gram-negative organisms. Tetracycline is used to treat acne and other skin infections, respiratory tract infections such as pneumonia, genital and urinary infections, and Helicobacter pylori (the bacteria that can lead to stomach ulcers) infection.

"Chlortetracycline" is the first drug in the tetracycline family and introduced in 1948. Overuse of tetracycline (and other antibiotics) in humans and farm animals has allowed some bacteria to build up a resistance to antibiotics.

As per the IP: Tetracycline ($C_{22}H_{24}N_2O_8$) capsules should not contain less than 88.0% of tetracycline.

PREPARATION OF TETRACYCLINE CAPSULES

Table 7.1 Tetracycline capsules formulation table.

S. No	Ingredients	Quantity given	Quantity taken
1.	Tetracycline hydrochloride	250mg	
2.	Starch	25mg	
3.	Talcum	25mg	

A. Filling of capsule:

1. Weigh the required quantity of drug and other excipients.
2. Talcum and Starch should be free from moisture, dry and sieved through sieve no.#100.
3. Mix all the ingredients uniformly using mortar and pestle and glass rod.
4. Take "0" number empty capsule shells for filling of content using hand operated filling machine.
5. Hand operated filling machine consists of beds, loading tray, powder tray, pin plate, sealing plate, lever, a cam handle.

B. Filling of capsule by capsule machine:

1. The empty capsules are filled in the loading tray and placed over the bed.
2. Separate the capsules cap from their bodies using cam handle.
3. Then powder tray is filled with an accurate quantity of drug mixture with the help of scraper and place over the bed containing capsules bodies.
4. The pin plate is lowered using lever and filled the drug mixture into the bodies of the capsules.
5. Again, place the cap holding tray over the filled bodies capsules.
6. Lock the cap and bodies of capsules using lever. Collect the filled capsules.

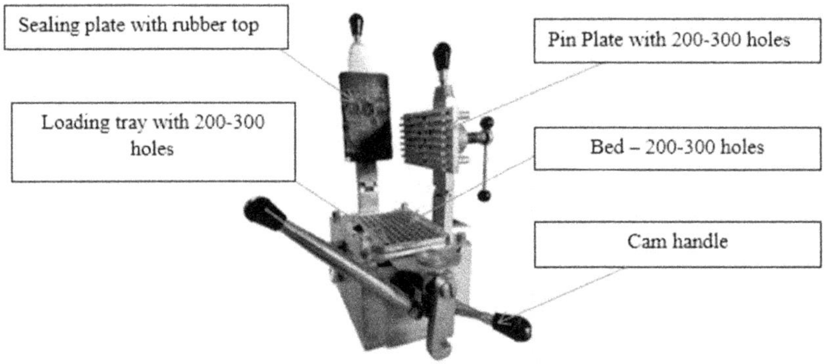

Fig 7.1 Capsule filling machine.

Packing: Blister packaging or closed container with screw cap is used.

Storage: Store in tightly closed container and placed in cool and dry place.

Instructions:

1. Stop using medicine who have shown allergic reaction to tetracycline drug.
2. Avoid giving tetracycline with penicillin or other antibacterial.
3. Precautions should be taken in patients with anticoagulant therapy.

Use: Tetracycline is a broad-spectrum antibiotic, used to treat many diseases such as cholera, bronchitis, pneumonia, rickettsia infection.

Labelling

Ingredient list		**Mfg Lic No.**
	Formulation name	**Mfg date**
	(Quantity)	**Batch no.**
Use	**Antibiotic capsules**	**Exp. Date**
	External/Internal Use only	
Storage		**Name of manufacturer**
Instruction		

Evaluation methods for tetracycline capsules:

1. Evaluation of appearance, dimension, hardness, friability is performed as per the procedure mentioned in Experiment 3.
2. **Weight uniformity:** Weigh 20 intact capsule of tetracycline. Take one capsule and remove the contents completely on a butter paper. Now,

weigh empty shell and its content separately, finally calculate the amount of content by subtracting the weight of intact capsule minus weight of empty shell. Repeat the procedure for 19 capsule and calculate average weight of capsule content. Not more than two of the individual weights deviate from average weight and percentage deviation shown in table 7.2:

Table 7.2 Weights percentage deviation.

Average weight of capsule contents	% deviation
Less than 300mg	10
300mg or more	7.5

3. **Disintegration Time:** Place one tablet in each of tube of disintegrating apparatus. Suspend the disintegrating tubes in the beaker containing 900mL of distilled water. The basket raises and lowers in the medium with the help of motor for 15 minutes, at the frequency of 29-32 cycles/min and at temperature should be maintained at 37±2°C.
4. **Uniformity of content:** Randomly select 10 intact capsules and determine the active ingredient using method mentioned in monograph. The capsules comply with the test, if 9 out of 10 within the requirement of ±15% (85%-115%) limits and the tenth tablet is not outside ±25% (75%-125%) so the batch should be accepted. While if 2 capsules out of 10 falls outside the range ±15% so take 20 capsules and assay them individually and take the average of 30 capsules, so the requirements are met if 27 capsules in the ±15% range and only 3 capsules in the ±25% range.
5. **Dissolution test:** The release rate of Tetracycline hydrochloride from capsule is determine by Type-I (Paddle) dissolution apparatus(IP). The dissolution test is perform using 900mL of distilled water at 37ºC±0.5ºC and 75 rpm. A sample (10mL) of the solution is withdrawn from the dissolution apparatus, in every 10 mins (10, 20, 30, 40, 50 and 60 mins) and the samples is replaced with fresh dissolution medium (distilled water). The withdrawn sample is filtered through a 0.45μ membrane filter. Absorbance of these samples are measure at 276 nm using a UV double-beam spectrophotometer. Cumulative percentage drug release is calculated using an equation obtained from a standard curve (refer experiment 3).

Observations:

S. No	Test	Specification	Observation
1.	Coating	uniform/ non-uniform	
2.	Surface	smooth/ rough	
3.	Glossy	absent/ present	
4.	Cracks	Absent/ present	

Evaluation of tetracycline capsule

S. No	Sample	Dimensions	Weight (mg)	Disintegration time (min)	%Drug Content Release	Concentration (%)
1.						
2.						
3.						

Dissolution profile of tetracycline capsule

S. No	Sample	%Drug content Release (10min)	%Drug content Release (20min)	%Drug content Release (40min)	%Drug content Release (60min)	%Drug content Release (80min)	%Drug content Release (100min)
1.							
2.							
3.							

Result: The Tetracycline capsules were prepared and *pass or fail* the evaluation test as per IP

QUESTIONS

Q.1 What is the purpose of using Tetracycline HCl capsules?

Q.2 What is the component of capsules?

Q.3 Discuss the size of capsules.

Q.4 What are hard gelatin capsules?

Q.5 What are the quality control tests used for capsules?

Q.6 Name the diluents used in capsules formulations?

Q.7 What are soft gelatin capsules?

Answers on page.no: 89

CHAPTER 8

PREPARATION OF CALCIUM GLUCONATE INJECTION

Aim: To prepare and submit three ampoules of 10 mL calcium gluconate injection.

Requirements:

1. **Apparatus Required:** Beaker, measuring cylinder, syringe, needle, ampoules, whatman filter paper/membrane filter, autoclave.
2. **Chemical Required:** Calcium gluconate, calcium D -saccharate, water for injection.

Theory:

From the Greek word Para enteron, which meaning avoid the intestine, the word "parenteral" is derived. Due to their administration method of directly injecting into human tissues through the skin and mucous membranes, these dosage forms are distinct.

Parenteral products are sterile liquids or formulations with one or more active pharmaceutical ingredient that are injected, infused, or implanted into the body. These medications are dispense in sterile containers such as vials, ampules, and prefilled syringes. Parenteral formulations can be administered via four different routes: intradermal (IM), subcutaneous (SQ), intramuscular (IM), and intravenous (IV). For intravenous delivery, an active pharmaceutical ingredient or drug is dissolved, emulsified, or suspended in water for injection and administering by using a syringe and needle (injection) and keeping the patient comfortable and safe. Calcium gluconate is a calcium salt of gluconic acid, and can also be administered via parenteral route, as calcium supplement in bone related diseases such as osteoporosis, rickets, and in hyperkalemia. Calcium gluconate is white, crystalline, odourless granular powder, sparingly soluble in water but more soluble in boiling water. To prevent crystallization of calcium gluconate, 5% of calcium D-saccharate or calcium lactobionate is added as stabilizing agents in the calcium gluconate parenteral formulation.

As per the IP: calcium gluconate injection contains a quantity of calcium equivalent to not less than 8.5% and not more than 9.4 % of calcium gluconate.

Parenteral drug delivery has the following benefits:

a) They can bypass first-pass or pre-systemic metabolism and act quickly.
b) It is useful for administering drugs like insulin, hormones, antibiotics, and biological molecules that are ineffective orally or destroyed in gastric media.
c) It is used in patients who are unconscious, uncooperative, and vomiting patient or emergency condition that require rapid onset of action.
d) Deliver precise dose of medication with high bioavailability.
e) The drug action can be prolonged by modifying the formulation.

Limitations:

a) Pain is felt at the injection site.
b) The drug must be administered by qualified individuals.
c) Administering a medicine by the incorrect injection site can be lethal.
d) When a patient has an overdose, it becomes more challenging to save them.
e) A person may experience an allergic or sensitive reaction to a medication.

PREPARATION OF CALCIUM GLUCONATE INJECTION

Table 8.1 Calcium gluconate injection formulation table.

S. No	Ingredients	Quantity given for 100mL	Quantity taken for 30 mL
1.	Calcium gluconate	9.56mg	
2.	Calcium D-saccharate	0.35 g	
3.	Water for injection (q.s)	100 mL	

q.s=quantity sufficient

Procedure:

1. Calculate and weigh accurately the quantity of calcium gluconate and calcium D-saccharate as mentioned in table 8.1 and keep separately on the butter paper.

2. Take 100 mL beaker, dissolve prescribed quantity of calcium gluconate in water for injection.
3. To the above solution, add calcium D-saccharate, with continuous stirring.
4. Adjust the pH (6-8) of final solution with the help of 10% sodium hydroxide solution and filter it by using Whatman filter paper.
5. Fill the final preparation in the sterile ampoules with the help of syringe and seal the ampoules by pull-sealing technique
6. Sterilize the sealed ampules by autoclaving at 121°C for 30 minutes.

Packing: Ampoules are packed in a suitable ampoule box.

Storage: Store in a cool and dark place. If any foreign matter observed in the ampoule, discard the preparation.

Important Instruction:

1. Calcium gluconate injection is for intravenous use only.
2. The patient should be in the lying position and closely monitored during injection.
3. In case of any allergic reaction, constipation, increased urination consults your physician.

Labelling:

List of Ingredient		Mfg Lic No.
	Formulation name	Mfg date
	(Quantity)	Batch no.
Use	As Ca supplement/ in bone disorders	Exp. Date
	Internal Use only	
Storage		Name of manufacturer
Imp. Instruction		

Observation table

S.No		Name of the test	Specification	Observation
1.		Appearance	Clear	
2.		Leakage test	No leakage	

contd..

3.		pH	6-8	
4.		Odor	Odorless	

Result: Three ampoules of 10 ml each containing calcium gluconate injection were prepared, labelled and submitted.

QUESTION

Q.1 What is the use of calcium gluconate injection?

Q.2 Define stabilizing agent. Which stabilizing agent is used in Calcium gluconate injections?

Q.3 Name the filter used for sterile filtration?

Q.4 State the different methods of ampoule sealing?

Q.5 What do you understand by Water for injection (WFI)?

Answers on page.no: 90

CHAPTER 9

PREPARATION OF ASCORBIC ACID INJECTION

Aim: To prepare and submit two ampoules of 10 mL ascorbic acid injection IP.

Requirements:

1. **Apparatus required:** Ampoules, beaker, graduated cylinder, syringe needle (2mL), Whatman filter paper or G-4, pH paper/ pH meter, pipette.
2. **Chemicals required:** Ascorbic acid, sodium bicarbonate, p- choro meta cresol, water for injection.

Theory:

Injections are the sterile parenteral preparations used for systemic delivery of drug. These preparations are available in solutions, emulsion or suspension form. In the formulation of parental products, vehicles (Water for injections, oils, alcohols) and additives (solubilizing agents, stabilizers, buffering agents, antibacterial agents, chelating agents, suspending, emulsifying, wetting agents) are used. Ascorbic acid (vitamin C) is a water-soluble vitamin, and occurs as a white or slightly yellow crystal or powder with a slight acidic taste. It is a scurvy curing product. In the presence of light, air and heat, oxidation of vitamin C occurs and it acquire dark colour. Thus, to prevent the oxidation, ascorbic acid is stored in ambered coloured bottles. Ascorbic acid is freely soluble in water, sparingly soluble in alcohol and insoluble in chloroform, ether, and benzene. The empirical formula of vitamin C is $C_6H_8O_6$ and the molecular weight is 176.13. Ascorbic acid injection is a clear, colourless to slightly yellow sterile solution of ascorbic acid in Water for Injection, intended for intravenous, intramuscular, or subcutaneous route of administration.

The structure of Ascorbic acid (vitamin C) is as follows:

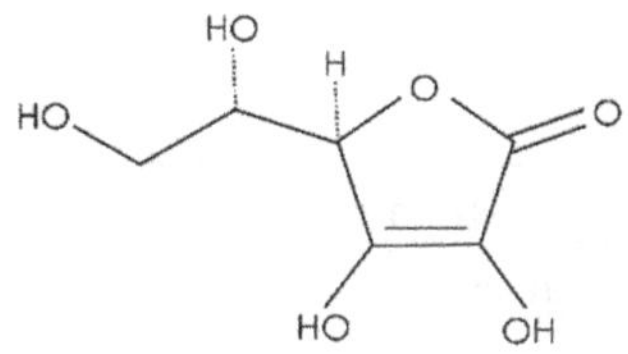

As per the I.P- Ascorbic acid injection contains not less than 95.0 per cent and not more than 115.0 % of the amount of ascorbic acid.

PREPARATION OF ASCORBIC ACID INJECTION

Table 9.1 Ascorbic acid injection formulation table.

S. No	Ingredients	Quantity for 100ml	Quantity taken
1.	Ascorbic acid	25.00 g	
2.	Sodium bicarbonate	14.58 g	
3.	p- chloro meta cresol	0.1 g	
4.	Water for injection (q.s)	100ml	

q.s=quantity sufficient

Procedure:

1. Calculate and weigh the required quantity of ingredients (table 9.1).
2. Clean the ampoules with sterilized water and dry it.
3. In a 100ml beaker, add ascorbic acid with $2/3^{rd}$ volume of Water for injection (WFI) with continuous stirring.
4. To the above beaker add sodium bicarbonate which produces effervescence in the solution, that help in dissolving the ascorbic acid.
5. Continue the stirring till ascorbic acid completely dissolved.
6. With the help of pipette, add p-chloro meta cresol to above solution.
7. Adjust the pH (5-7) of final solution with 10% sodium hydroxide solution and filter the solution using whatman filter paper.
8. Transfer the solution to sterile ampoule with the help of syringe, seal the tip using pull sealing technique.
9. Sterilize the sealed ampoules by autoclaving at 121°c for 30 minutes.

Packing: Packed in light resistant ampoule box.

Storage: Store between 2°C to 8°C. Keep away from children and light. Do not allow to stand at room temperature before use.

Uses: Ascorbic acid Injection is recommended in the treatment of scurvy.

Labelling:

Ingredient list		Mfg Lic No.
	Formulation name	Mfg date
	(Quantity)	Batch no.
Use	In Scurvy/ Vit. C deficiency	Exp. Date
	Internal Use only	
Storage		Name of manufacture
Imp. Instruction		

Observation table

S. No	Name of the test	Specification	Observation
1.	Appearance	Clear	
2.	Leakage test	No leakage	
3.	pH	5-7	
4.	Odor	Odorless	

Result: Two ampoules of ascorbic acid injections were prepared, labelled and submitted.

QUESTIONS

Q.1 What do you understand by Injection?

Q.2 Why drugs are given in injectable form?

Q.3 What is the use of ascorbic acid?

Q.4 What are the route of administration for ascorbic acid injection?

Q.5 What is Water for Injection?

Q.6 Why additives are used in the parenteral preparations?

Q.7 What is isotonicity?

Q.8 Write examples of tonicity modifier?

Answers on page.no: 90

CHAPTER 10

PREPARATION OF ATROPINE SULPHATE EYE DROPS

Aim: To Prepare and submit 15mL Atropine sulphate eye drops IP

Requirements:

1. **Apparatus Required:** Beaker, glass stirring rod, measuring cylinder, autoclave, spatula.
2. **Chemical Required:** Atropine sulphate, phenyl mercuric nitrate, sulphuric acid, distilled water.

Theory:

Ophthalmic preparations are the sterile products, essentially free from foreign particles, formulated and packaged in suitable container for ophthalmic use. Eye drops are sterile aqueous or oily solutions or suspension of one or more medicaments intended for installation into the conjunctival sac for therapeutic purposes. Some eye drops before use need to be reconstituted in an appropriate sterile water. In such cases the label should state clearly on the container 'Powder for eye drop' and should include directions for the use of eye drops. Aqueous eye drops contain suitable antimicrobial preservatives at the appropriate concentrations because they are intended for use more than once. Atropine sulphate eye drop is an ophthalmic sterile solution containing 1% of atropine sulphate and used to dilate the pupil before eye examination, in the treatment of eye problems such as amblyopia (lazy eyes) and cycloplegia. Anticholinergic Atropine sulphate relaxes the ciliary muscle of the eye and causes dilation of pupil (mydriasis).

Structure of Atropine Sulphate:

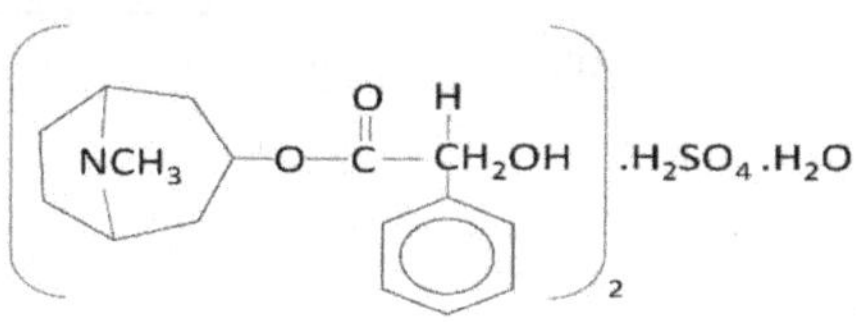

PREPARATION OF ATROPINE SULPHATE EYE DROPS

Table 10.1 Atropine sulphate eye drops formulation table.

S. No	Ingredients	Quantity given for 100ml	Quantity taken
1.	Atropine sulphate	1 gm	
2.	Phenyl mercuric nitrate	0.002 gm	
3.	Distillation water (q.s)	100 mL	

q.s=quantity sufficient

Procedure:

1. Calculate and weigh all the ingredients required for eye drop, (table 10.1) and keep separately on the butter paper.
2. Take 50 mL beaker and dissolve atropine sulphate in 3/4 volume of distilled water, then add specified quantity of phenyl mercuric nitrate.
3. Adjust the pH (3.5 - 6.0) of preparation using 10% dil. sulphuric acid, make up the final volume with distilled water.
4. Clarify the resulting solution by passing through membrane filter.
5. Sterilize the product by autoclaving at 121°C for 30 minutes.

Packing: Store in sterile plastic dropper bottles.

Storage: Store below 25°C and keep away from the light and children.

Uses: 1. For pupil dilation (mydriasis).
2. It helps to restore the natural permeability of iris and ciliary of eyes.
3. To reduce inflammation of the anterior segment in case of iridocyclitis and anterior uveitis.

Instructions: 1. Wash hands before use.
2. For external use only.
3. Use within one month after opening of bottle.

Labelling:

Ingredient list		Mfg Lic No.
	Formulation name	Mfg date
	(Quantity)	Batch no.
Use	As mydriatic & for amblyopia	Exp. Date
	External/Internal Use only	
Storage		Name of manufacturer
Instruction		

Observation:

S. No	Name of the test	Specification	Observation
1.	Appearance	Clear, colourless	
2.	pH	3.5 - 6.0	
3.	Clarity test	Free from particulate matter	
4.	Sterility test	Sterile	

Result: 15mL Atropine sulphate eye drops were prepared, labelled and submitted.

QUESTION

Q.1 Why dilute sulphuric acid is used in the preparation of Atropine sulphate eye drop?

Q.2 Enlist the ingredients used in ophthalmic preparations?

Q.3 What are the ideal features of eye drops?

Q.4 Which are the commonly used preservatives in the preparation of eye drops?

Answers on page.no: 91

CHAPTER 11

PREPARATION OF ZINC SULPHATE EYE DROPS

Aim: To Prepare and submit 10 ml of Zinc Sulphate Eye Drops (IP)

Requirements:

1. **Apparatus Required:** Beaker, glass stirring rod, measuring cylinder, autoclave, spatula.
2. **Chemical Required:** Zinc sulphate, phenyl mercuric nitrate, sterile purified water.

Theory:

Eye drops are sterile ophthalmic preparations (saline or oily solutions or suspension containing one or more medicaments) that are free from foreign particles meant for topical application on eye (ocular route). It is administered to the eyelids or instillation into the cu-de-sac between the eyeball and eyelids. Saline eye drops are used to provide lubrication and tear replacing solutions. Certain eye drops contain drugs like steroids, antihistamines, sympathomimetics, nonsteroidal anti-inflammatory drugs (NSAIDs), antibiotics, antifungal to treat infectious eye diseases. If it is in powder form, then should be reconstituted in an appropriate sterile liquid immediately before use. Such eye drop formulation is clearly labelled with 'Powder for eye drop' and includes the direction. Eye drops should be isotonic with lachrymal secretion. Aqueous eye drops should contain suitable antimicrobial preservatives at the appropriate concentrations to prevent microbial growth on using multiple times. Zinc act as an antiseptic and astringent, used in the treatment of angular conjunctivitis) and other eye infections. Atropine sulphate eye drop is another example, specially used before eye examination and other eye conditions (cycloplegia).

PREPARATION OF ZINC SULPHATE EYE DROPS

Table 11.1 Zinc sulphate eye drops formulation table.

S. No	Ingredients	Quantity for 100ml	Quantity taken
1.	Zinc sulphate	0.25gm	
2.	Phenyl mercuric nitrate	0.002gm	
3.	Purified water (q.s)	100ml	

q.s. = Quantity sufficient

Procedure:

1. Clean and rinse all the glassware with sterile water.
2. Weight all the ingredients (table 11.1) and keep them separately.
3. Take 100 ml beaker and dissolve required quantity of phenyl mercuric nitrate in sufficient purified water.
4. Add zinc sulphate to the above solution with continue stirring.
5. Filter the solution through sintered glass funnel.
6. Transfer the final solution to the measuring cylinder and makeup the final volume by adding purified water.
7. Transfer in suitable container and sterile the preparation by autoclaving at 121°C for 30 minutes.

Packing: Packed in vertical fluted bottle made from glass or plastic.

Storage: Store in a cool place and keep away from sunlight and children.

Instruction: During the use, if irritation occurs, discontinue and consult your physician.

Uses: 1. To induce mydriasis and cycloplegia.

2. Used before eye examination, to dilate the pupil of eye

Labelling:

Ingredient list		**Mfg Lic No.**
	Formulation name	**Mfg date**
	(Quantity)	**Batch no.**
Use		**Exp. Date**
	External/Internal Use only	
Storage		**Name of manufacturer**
Instructions		

Observation Table:

S. No	Name of the test	Specification	Observation
1.	Appearance	Clear, colorless	
2.	pH	5-6	
3.	Clarity test	Free from particulate matter	
4.	Sterility test	Sterile	

Result: 10 mL Zinc sulphate eye drops has been prepared, labelled and submitted.

QUESTIONS

Q.1 What is the category of zinc sulphate eye drop?

Q.2 What are the important instructions given on the label?

Q.3 Which types of containers are used for ophthalmic preparations?

Q.4 What are the advantages of eye drops?

Q.5 What is the role of methyl paraben in eye drops?

Q.6 What are the components of eye drop preparation?

Q.7 What is the role of viscosity enhancer, buffer in the eye drop formulation?

Q.8 Write example of preservative agent used in eye preparation?

Q.9 What is the use of zinc sulphate eye drop?

Answers on page.no: 91

CHAPTER 12

PREPARATION OF EYE OINTMENT

Aim: To Prepare and submit 4gm of eye ointment.

Requirements:

1. **Apparatus required:** Beaker, glass rod, measuring cylinder, water bath, spatula, thermometer.
2. **Chemical required:** White soft paraffin, wool fat, liquid paraffin.

Theory:

Ophthalmic preparation is the sterile dosage form meant for topical application on eye. These preparations are prepared in an aseptic environmental condition by using suitable sterile containers. Ingredients used in ophthalmic dosage form should be non-irritating, free from grittiness and melt near the body temperature to ease the diffusion of drug through the lachrymal secretion of eye. Ophthalmic ointments tend to keep the drug in contact with the eye for longer duration than the suspension and solutions. Anhydrous Lanoline is added to the preparation to enhance dissolution process. Ophthalmic ointments are applied on the edges of the eyelids. In the preparation of eye ointment, soft white paraffin, wool fat and liquid paraffin are used as base. Chloramphenicol ointment, Tetracycline ointment, Hydrocortisone ointment are few examples of eye ointment.

PREPARATION OF EYE OINTMENT

Table 12.1 Eye ointment formulation table.

S. No	Ingredients	Quantity for 100 gm	Quantity taken
1.	White soft paraffin	80 gm	
2.	Wool fat (lanoline)	10 gm	
3.	Liquid paraffin	10 ml	

Procedure:

1. Weigh the required quantity of white soft paraffin, wool fat and keep them in a crucible.
2. Melt the ingredient of crucible on the water bath.
3. Add prescribed quantity of liquid paraffin to the above preparation with continuous stirring.
4. Remove the crucible from the water bath and keep stirring until semisolid texture is formed, cool the preparation.
5. Transfer the prepared ointment to a suitable sterile container.

Packing: Store in aluminum tube with screw cape made of polyethylene.

Dose: Apply eye ointment every three hours.

Storage: Stored at the temperature of 25°C or below 25°C and keep away from light.

Instructions:

1. Keep the medicine out of the sight and reach of children.
2. Dispose the ointment tube when treatment is over.
3. Use within one month after opening of container.
4. Do not touch the tip of tube, to avoid contamination.
5. External use only

Uses: 1. Reduce soreness in dry eye.

2. Treat inflammation and irritation occur during eye problem.

Labelling:

Ingredient list		Mfg Lic No.
	Formulation name	Mfg date
	(Quantity)	Batch no.
Use		Exp. Date
	External/Internal Use only	
Storage		Company name
Imp. Instruction		

Observation table

S. No	Name of the test	Specification	Observation
1.	Appearance	Pale yellow color	
2.	Leakage test	No leakage	
3.	pH	6-8	
4.	Homogeneity	Homogeneous and uniform consistency	
5.	Texture	Smooth	
6.	Spread ability	Easily spreadable	

Result: 4 gm of eye ointment was prepared and submitted

QUESTION

Q.1 What is the role of soft white paraffin and liquid paraffin in eye ointment preparation?

Q.2 What is the role of wool fat in the preparation of eye ointment?

Q.3 What is the purpose of using eye ointment?

Q.4 What is Conjunctivitis?

Answers on page.no: 92

CHAPTER 13

PREPARATION OF COLD CREAM

Aim: To prepare and submit 10g of cold cream.

Requirements:

1. **Apparatus Required:** Beaker, glass rod, china dish, mortar and pestle, thermometer.
2. **Chemicals Required**: White bees wax, liquid paraffin, borax, purified water, perfume.

Theory:

Topical delivery is the application of a drug-containing formulation on the skin to treat dermatological problems such as psoriasis. The aim of topical dosage form is to administer the pharmacologically active drug directly to the surface of skin for its maximum therapeutic effect. Semisolid dosage form is meant for topical application. A cream is a homogenous semisolid preparation intended for external or topical application. It exists in two forms: oil-in-water (O/W) creams, in which small droplets of oil are dispersed in a continuous water phase, and water-in-oil (W/O) creams, in which small droplets of water are dispersed in a continuous oily phase.

Cold cream is a water-in-oil type emulsion, that provide emollient effect to the skin. The main activity of the cold cream is to slow the rate of evaporation. It is ideal for treating dry skin on knees, elbows and feet, and is also used as a natural makeup remover. The combination of fat (beeswax) and water helps to moisturise the skin. Borax and bees wax are the main components of cream, and they act as emulsifying agents. Lanolin is used in cold cream as lubricating agent and liquid paraffin or petroleum jelly are used as cleanser.

PREPARATION OF COLD CREAM

Table 13.1 Cold cream formulation table.

Ingredients	**Quantity for 100 gm**	**Quantity required**
Oil Phase		
Mineral oil	50 g	
Bees wax	16 gm	
Aqueous Phase		
Borax	0.8 g	
Purified water	33 ml	
Perfume (Rose water)	q.s	
Propyl paraben	0.02 g	
Methyl paraben	0.18 g	

q.s. = Quantity sufficient

Procedure:

1. To prepare the oil phase, start by grating the white beeswax into small pieces. Weigh the required quantity of white beeswax, propyl paraben and liquid paraffin in a100 ml beaker and melt them on a water bath with temperature set upto 40-70°C.
2. To prepare aqueous phase, take prescribed quantity (table 13.1) of borax, methyl paraben and purified water in a 100 ml beaker and heat at 70°C to make clear solution.
3. Add aqueous phase to the oily phase slowly while maintaining the temperature at 70°C under continuous stirring.
4. Stir continuously at room temperature, until it cools down. When the temperature lowers to 40-45°C, add rose oil and mix uniformly, until a homogenous semi solid mass is obtained.
5. Transfer the homogenous mass to the suitable container.

Packing: Store in a wide mouth container with screw cap.

Storage: Store in a cool place, but do not allow to freeze.

Uses: 1. Cold cream is used as an emollient for the treatment of dry skin.

2. It is also used to treat skin disease like eczema and psoriasis.

Labelling:

Ingredient list		Mfg Lic No.
	Formulation name	Mfg date
	(Quantity)	Batch no.
Use		Exp. Date
	External/Internal Use only	
Storage		Company name
Imp. Instruction		

Observation table

S. No	Name of the test	Specification	Observation
1.	Appearance	White	
2.	Odour	Rose type	
3.	pH	5-6	
4.	Homogeneity	Homogeneous and uniform consistent	
5.	Texture	Smooth	
6.	Spread ability	Easily spreadable	
7.	Type of smear	Non- greasy	
8.	Emolliency	No residue left	
9.	Washability	Easily washable	

Result: 10gm of cold cream was prepared and submitted in a well labelled closed container.

QUESTIONS

Q.1 What is the difference between ointments and creams?

Q.2 What is the use of liquid paraffin in cold cream?

Q.3 What is cold cream?

Q.4 what is emulsion?

Q.5 What is an emulsifying agent?

Answers on page.no: 92

CHAPTER 14

PREPARATION OF VANISHING CREAMS

Aim: To prepare and submit 30gm of vanishing cream.

Requirements:

1. **Apparatus required:** Beaker, measuring cylinder, glass rod, sieve no. 60 #, thermometer.
2. **Chemicals required:** Stearic acid, glycerin, lanoline, purified water, triethanolamine, methyl paraben, propyl paraben, rose water.

Theory:

A cream is a semisolid emulsion dosage form intended for external application. It exists in two form: oil-in-water (O/W) creams, in which small droplets of oil are dispersed in a continuous water phase and water-in-oil (W/O) creams, in which small droplets of water are dispersed in a continuous oily phase. Oil-in-water creams are more comfortable and cosmetically acceptable as they are less greasy and easily washed off. Water-in-oil creams are more difficult to handle due to their greasy nature.

"Vanishing cream" as its name, disappear within minutes upon application and provide smooth emollient base to the skin. Vanishing cream is an o/w type emulsion and cold cream is w/o type emulsion. Vanishing creams are also called foundation cream to help face powder to adhere on the skin surface. They protect the skin from the surrounding environment and provide a non-greasy texture to normal to oily skin, which makes them suitable for summer days. Glycerin as humectant is added to the cream preparation to prevent cracking of cream by reducing loss of water from it and to improve skin's hydration. By reducing moisture loss, it helps skin to look fresh and elegant. In the preparation of vanishing cream, lanolin provides sufficient moisture to the skin, glycerin used as humectant, stearic acid gives consistency and shinning appearance to the cream and perfume such as lavender oil, sandal wood oil adds fragrance to the preparation.

Purified water is used as solvent medium and provides stability to the preparation. Hard water contains some ions like magnesium and calcium which cause inversion of emulsion. Hydroquinone is one of the most common constituents of vanishing cream used to lighten the dark spots of skin. Hydroquinone (4%) is added to vanishing cream to reduce unnecessary dark spots or discoloration on the skin.

Synonym: Foundation cream, face cream

PREPARATION OF VANISHING CREAM

Table 14.1 Vanishing cream formulation table.

S. No	Ingredients	Quantity for 100 gm	Quantity taken
1.	Stearic acid	18 gm	
2.	Glycerin	3 gm	
3.	Lanoline	2 gm	
4.	Triethonalamine	1 gm	
5.	Methyl paraben	0.18 gm	
6.	Propyl paraben	0.02 gm	
7.	Rose water	q.s	
8.	Purified water	75.8 mL	

q.s= Quantity sufficient

Procedure:

1. Weigh all the prescribe ingredients of the varnishing cream properly mentioned in table 14.1 and keep them separately on a butter paper.
2. Take stearic acid and lanoline in a beaker (250mL) and melt them at 60°C using water bath.
3. In another beaker (250mL), add required quantity of glycerin, triethanolamine and water. Heat upto 60^0C (temperature should be maintained by using thermometer).
4. Add the preparation of the first beaker to the second beaker drop by drop with continuous stirring.
5. After cooling of above mixture, add methyl paraben, propyl paraben, rose oil and mix them thoroughly to obtain uniform product.

Packing: Store in wide mouth container with screw cap

Storage: Store at cool temperature (preferably below 25°C) and in dry place. Do not freeze.

Uses: 1. It helps to keep the skin moisturized.
2. Used as base for cosmetics and make-up.
3. Skin looks fresh and elegant.
4. Provide a sheen effect to the skin.

Labelling:

Ingredient list		**Mfg Lic No.**
	Formulation name	**Mfg date**
	(Quantity)	**Batch no.**
Use		**Exp. Date**
	External/Internal Use only	
Storage		**Company name**
Imp. Instruction		

Observation table

S. No	Name of the test	Specification	Observation
1.	Appearance	White	
2.	Odour	Rose type	
3.	pH	5-6	
4.	Homogeneity	Homogeneous and uniform consistent	
5.	Texture	Smooth	
6.	Spreadability	Easily spreadable	
7.	Type of smear	Non- greasy	
8.	Emolliency	No residue left	
9.	Washability	Easily washable	

Result: 30 gm of Vanishing cream was prepared and submitted in well labelled closed container.

QUESTIONS

Q.1 What is the reason for adding methyl and propyl paraben in the vanishing cream?

Q.2 Define Vanishing cream?

Q.3 Why triethanolamine is used in the preparation of a cream?

Q.4 What are the substitutes of triethanolamine?

Q.5 What is humectant?

Q.6 Why alkali is added to the cream preparations?

Answers on page.no: 93

CHAPTER 15

EVALUATION OF GLASS CONTAINER

Aim: To evaluate glass containers as per IP (Indian Pharmacopoeia)

Requirements:

1. **Apparatus required:** Borosilicate glass bottles, petri dishes, autoclave, pipette (2mL), conical flask (250mL)
2. **Chemicals required:** Methyl red solution, distilled water, 0.01M HCl

Theory:

Packaging plays an important role in storage, transportation and safekeeping of the manufactured product. Choosing the appropriate packaging for the product is crucial for its stability. A package includes the container that holds the product and a closure that seals the container to keep out moisture, bacteria, and gases like carbon dioxide and oxygen etc. Containers are integral part of packaging, for storage, transportation of formulation, identification and use. These containers are designed not only ensure medication safety and efficacy, but also prevent pharmaceutical products from tampering, ingestion by children and counterfeit medications. In pharmaceutical industry, packaging material of containers and closures plays vital role in maintaining the stability of formulations. Packaging provides protection, presentation, identification, information, and convenience to encourage patient compliance during therapy. Common container types include well closed, single dose, multi dose and light resistant containers. Commonly used material for containers are: glass, plastic, metal or paper in addition to a *closure* that may include cork, glass, plastic, metal, or rubber. Ideally, a good packaging should be able to provide sufficient strength to withstand shocks of handling, leakage of product, protect against environmental conditions like light, air, and moisture, prevent permeability of gases and should not interact physically or chemically with the contents.

Glass is the most preferable choice as a container material. Glass is composed of silica (59-80%) with varying degree of calcium oxide (5-12 %), sodium oxide (12-17 %), aluminum oxide (0.5-3.0 %), barium oxide, boric oxide, potassium oxide, and magnesium oxide. The high melting point of glass is due to the presence of silica. The melting point and viscosity of the glass is modified by the addition of oxides. According to the composition, there are four types of glass containers:

1. Type I (borosilicate glass),
2. Type II (treated soda lime glass),
3. Type III (soda lime glass),
4. Type IV (general purpose soda lime glass).

During storage of water containing preparation, exchange of ions takes place between glass (Na^+) and aqueous component (H^+), causing alkali leaching and increases the pH (alkalinity), which affect the strength of container and stability of pharmaceutical preparation. Type I and Type II glass containers have good hydrolytic resistance due to surface treatment with sulphur dioxide or alkalizers to neutralize the inner surface of glass container, which lowers the concentration of migratory oxide into the pharmaceutical preparation.

Table 15.1 Type of glass containers and their properties.

S. No	Type of glass containers	Properties	Uses
1.	Type I borosilicate glass	Withstand at high temperatures, high hydrolytic resistant, low leachability, low thermal coefficient of expansion	Laboratory glass apparatus, storing WFI and parenteral preparations
2.	Type II treated soda-lime glass	high hydrolytic and chemically resistant	alkali-sensitive products, infusion fluids, blood and plasma
3.	Type III regular soda-lime glass	moderate hydrolytic resistant	dry powder, oleaginous solutions
4.	Type IV (NP) general purpose soda-lime glass {NP-non-parenteral}	low hydrolytic resistant	oral and topical products

Table.15.2 Specification of hydrolytic resistance test.

Nominal capacity of container(ml)	Number of containers to be used	Volume of test solution to be used for titration(ml)
Up to 3	at least 20	25
5 or less	At least 10	50
6 to 30	At least 5	50
More than 30	At least 3	100

Procedure:

Hydrolytic resistance test (as per I.P 2014)

1. The number of containers to be examine and volume of test solution for the determination of hydrolytic resistance test are given in table 15.2.
2. Clean and rinse each new glass container with freshly prepared distilled water at least three times at room temperature.
3. Fill the container to the brim with freshly prepared distilled water, empty it and calculate the average overflow volume (AOV).
4. a) For ampoules, fill them with freshly prepared distilled water to the maximum volume and seal them by fusion technique.

   b) For bottles or vials, fill the distilled water upto the 90% of AOV and cover them with borosilicate glass dishes or aluminum foil.
5. Place the containers (ampoules or bottles or vials) in an autoclave. Remove air by injecting steam for 10 min. Raise the temperature to about 100 °C to 121 °C for 20 min. Maintain the temperature of 121°C for next 60 min. After 60 min, reduce the temperature from 121 °C to 100 °C for 40 min.
6. Remove the containers from the autoclave and cool under running tap water. After cooling, carry out the titration with 0.01 M HCl within one hour of removing the containers from the autoclave.
7. Collect and combine the contents from all containers. Take the volume of test solution as specified in Table 15.2, transfer it to the conical flask, add 0.15 ml of methyl red indicator and note the end point when yellow colour turns into pink on titrating with 0.01M HCl.
8. Repeat step 7 for blank (distilled water). Calculate and compare the amount of HCl consumed by test solution and blank solution. The volume of HCl should not exceed the limit that is mentioned in Indian Pharmacopoeia (Table 15.3).

Table 15.3 Volume of HCl required for different capacity glass containers.

S. No	Capacity of container (corresponding to 90% average overflow volume (ml)	Volume of 0.01 M HCL for 100 ml of Test solution	
		Type I or II Glass (ml)	Type III Glass (ml)
1.	Not more than 1	2.0	20.0
2.	More than 1 but not more than 2	1.8	17.6
3.	More than 2 but not more than 5	1.3	13.2
4.	More than 5 but not more than 10	1.0	10.0
5.	More than 10 but not more than 20	0.80	8.1
6.	More than 20 but not more than 50	0.60	6.1
7.	More than 50 but not more than 100	0.50	4.8
8.	More than 100 but not more than 200	0.40	3.8
9.	More than 200 but not more than 500	0.30	2.9
10.	More than 500	0.20	2.2

Observations

1. Capacity of each container in mL =________________mL
2. Volume of 0.01HCl required for 100ml of liquid from container i.e. sample (X) =______________mL
3. Volume of 0.01HCl required for 100ml of distilled water i.e blank (Y) =_____________mL

Calculations:

Volume of 0.01M HCl required for test solution (X-Y) in mL=______mL

Result: The given glass containers pass/fail the hydrolytic resistance test as per I.P standard.

QUESTIONS

Q.1 Describe the features of container?

Q.2 Why colorants are used in glass containers?

Q.3 Give examples of colorants used in glass containers?

Q.4 What is water attack test?

Q.5 What is hydrolytic resistance?

Q.6 What do you understand by packaging?

Q.7 What is the difference between primary, secondary and tertiary packaging?

Answers on page.no: 93

ANSWERS TO ALL CHAPTERS

CHAPTER 1

1. The objective of Preformulation studies is to develop reliable and competent dosage form, by providing drug release kinetic profile, drug interaction profile with ingredients and physico-chemical parameter of reported drug.
2. The Physico-chemical parameter of the new drug helps in determining the physical characteristics (particle size, density) and kinetic rate profile, which helps in formulation of dosage form.
3. Bulk characterization determines the crystallinity and polymorphism nature of drug. It includes particle size, bulk density, and surface morphology.
4. It is the physical description of the drug substance including colour, odor, and taste.
5. Hygroscopy can be defined as the capacity of a material to absorb atmospheric moisture.
6. X- ray differential scanning microscopy, differential thermal analysis, hot stage microscopy, scanning electron microscopy (SEM) and transmission electron microscopy (TEM) are the techniques used for analysis of drug form.
7. Density can be defined as ratio of mass of a substance to its volume, which greatly depends on particle size distribution and shape.
   - (a) **TRUE DENSITY-** it is defined as a particle's mass divided by its volume, excluding open and closed pores.
   - (b) **BULK DENSITY-** it is defined as total volume occupied by entire powder mass.
   - (c) **TAPPED DENSITY-** it is defined by placing graduated cylinder containing known weight of sample on tapped density apparatus and is operated for the fixed number of taps until a constant volume is attained.
8. Partition coefficient (log P) is defined as the proportion of a analyte concentrations in a mixture of two immiscible solvents (water and octanol) at equilibrium.

9. Angle of repose can be used to monitor the flow property of powder when the powder/granules particles are smooth and round, the angle of repose is low and if particles are fine and sticky, the angle of repose is high.
10. Tapped density helps in predicting the cohesiveness of particles which affect the flowability of powder or granules.

Chapter 2

1. Starch is used as a disintegrating agent and absorbent.
2. Acetaminophen or Para-hydroxy acetanilide
3. Antipyretics are the drugs used to lower elevated body temperature in fever.
4. Lubricants are the excipient used to improve the flow property of granules and prevent sticking of material to the dies of compression machine during punching of tablets.
5. Talc, magnesium stearate, calcium stearate
6. 1. Binding
   2. Sticking
   3. Capping and lamination,
   4. Weight variation,
   5. Mottling,
   6. Hardness variation,
   7. Double impression.
7. Tablets are the solid unit tamper proof dosage form, which provide greatest precision and least content variability.
8. 1. Dose precision
   2. Easy to administered
   3. More stable
   4. Light and compact
   5. Economical

Chapter 3

1. Tablets are solid dosage forms each containing a unit dose of one or more medicament.
2. 1. The tablet should include the correct dose of the drug.
   2. The appearance of the tablet should be elegant, and its weight, size, and appearance should be consistent.

3. The drug should be released from the tablet in a controlled and reproducible way.
4. The tablet should be biocompatible with human body.

3. The amount of force needed to break a tablet is known as its tablet hardness. It measures the ability of tablet to withstand mechanical pressure during handling, packaging, storing and transportation.

4. A glidants is a substance that is added to a powder to improve its flowability within the range of concentration (0.1 - 1% w/w).

5. A compressed tablet is formed by applying enough pressure to dry granular powders that causes the particles to come together and produce tablet.

6. Friability meaning crumble, friability test is performed to ensure the durability of tablet during handling, packaging, storing and transportation

7. The process by which a material turns into a solution is called dissolution. Dissolution test measures the rate and extent at which a solution forms from a dosage form (a pill, capsule, ointment). The dissolution of a drug is important for its bioavailability and therapeutic effectiveness.

8. Pfizer tablet hardness tester is a piler fitted with a pressure dial. The tablet is placed between the jaw of the piler and pressure is applied by pressing the handles with hand until the tablet break.

9. This test determines whether dosage forms such as tablets, capsules, pessaries and suppositories disintegrate within a prescribed time when placed in a liquid medium under the prescribed experimental conditions.

10. Uniformity of weight is an in-process test parameter which ensures consistency of dosage units during compression. Uniformity of weight is used for capsules and tablets.

CHAPTER 4

1. Hypodermic pills are small-scale, easily soluble, soft tablets made by molding method. These tablets are dissolved in a suitable in a suitable vehicle (water for injections) and administered by parental route.

2. 1. The drug should be uniformly distributed throughout the tablet.
   2. They should be accurate and uniform in weight.
   3. Its size and shape should be reasonable for easy to administration.
   4. It should be chemically and physically stable during storage.
   5. It should be attractive.

3. When the bridging liquid droplets are bigger than the original crystals, they penetrate the droplets and agglomerate with them, a phenomenon known as crystal bridging.

4. 1. Milling of drugs and excipients
   2. Mixing of powders, disintegrate and lubricant,
   3. Compression into tablet.

5. In the process of making tablets, dry granulation is often used for drugs that are heat- or moisture-sensitive. Dry granulation ensures the stability and potency of the active pharmaceutical ingredients (APIs) during the compression and storage stages by avoiding the need for liquid binders.

6. 1. Friability test, hardness test
   2. Uniformity of weight
   3. Uniformity of content
   4. Disintegration and dissolution test

7. Wet granulation method is used to produce granules of drug and excipient for following reasons:
   1. The size and shape of the grains ought to be consistent.
   2. Granules ought to flow freely.
   3. Granules ought to be robust enough to endure processing and handling.
   4. The granules should be compatible with the other ingredients in the formulation.

CHAPTER 5

1. Methods used for tablet coating
   1. Sugar Coating
   2. Film coating
   3. Enteric coating

4. Press or dry coating

2. 1. Increase in the weight of tablets or dosage form.
2. Steps of coating is more as compared to film coating.
3. Chipping and cracking of coating.
4. Poor distribution of coating liquid.

3. Hydroxy propyl methyl cellulose (HPMC), Methyl hydroxyethyl cellulose (MHEC), Shellac, Eudragit L and S.

4. Plasticizers are the compounds added to the polymer, to improve its processability, flexibility, and stretch ability. Plasticizer is added in the concentration of 5% to 35% w/w. Example: castor oil, spans, tween, PEG (200-400 MW) commonly used plasticizer.

5. *Steps* involved in *sugar Coating* of Tablets are: Sealing (Seal Coat), Sub-Coating, Smooth coating, Color coating, Polishing, Printing.

6. Colourants used in film coating are: Red Ferric Oxide, Titanium Oxide, Lead Oxide, Copper Sulfate, and Carbon Black.

7. Film coating is the process that involves the application of thin polymeric coating on the surface of tablet, granules, and pellets.

8. 1. Sticking and picking
2. Orange-Peel
3. Color variation
4. Cracking
5. Blistering
6. Hazing film
7. Brigding and filling

9. The solvent system is used to dissolve or disperse the polymer or other additives and convey them to the material surface.

Example: water, ethanol, methanol, chloroform, acetone

10. Inadequate spreading of the coating solution before drying causes bumpy or orange-peel effect on the surface of the tablet. Tablet has a matt appearance rather than a glossy texture and also occur due to high viscosity of coating solution.

CHAPTER 6

1. A tablet press is a mechanical device that compresses powder into tablets of uniform size and weight.

2. Different types of tablets are:

1. Coated Tablets
2. Enteric-Coated Tablets
3. Dispersible Tablets
4. Modified Release Tablets
5. Prolonged Release Tablets
6. Effervescent Tablets
7. Lozenges and Sublingual Tablets
8. Uncoated tablets

3. Enteric coated tablets are tablets that are coated with an enteric coating which protects the drug from acidic pH and enzymatic degradation in the stomach.

4. Methacrylate copolymers, hydroxypropyl methylcellulose acetate succinates and cellulose acetate phthalate are used as enteric polymers.

5. Disintegrates agents promote break-up of tablet into smaller fragments in an aqueous environment, which increase surface area and release of the drug substance.

6. Coating provides stability and mechanical strength to the tablets during handling, swallowing, and sticking.

7. Core tablets are prepared by direct compression method using disintegrating agent and coated with polymers like HPMC K100M, ethyl cellulose.

CHAPTER 7

1. Tetracycline HCl 250mg capsule is an antibiotic medicine, used to stop the growth of infection causing bacteria.

2. The empty capsule shells are made of gelatin, sugar, and water.

3. Capsules ranging in size from 000 (largest) to 5 (smallest).

4. Hard gelatin capsules are a type of capsule used to contain medicine in the form of dry powder or very small pellets. A hard gelatin capsule shell consists of two pieces: a cap and a body.

5. The hard and soft gelatin capsules should be subjected to following tests-Shape and size, colour thickness of capsule, disintegration test, weight variation test, and percentage of medicaments test.

6. Starch, lactose, mannitol, MCC (microcrystalline cellulose).

7. A soft gelatin capsule is a type of capsule that contains medicine in the form of liquid or powder, and dissolves more quickly than a hard gelatin capsule, these capsules are composed of gelatin, plasticizers, preservative, colouring and opacifying agents, flavouring agents and sugars.

CHAPTER 8

1. Calcium gluconate injection is used as supplement in bone related diseases such as osteoporosis, rickets, as well as in cardiac arrest.
2. Stabilizing agents are added to the pharmaceutical products to provide and preserve structure of drug, stability, and viscosity of preparation. calcium D-saccharate or calcium lactobionate is used as stabilizing agents in the calcium gluconate parenteral formulation.
3. Sintered glass filter is used for sterile filtration.
4. Different methods of ampoules sealing are as follows:

   (1) Tip seal **(2)** Pull seal
5. Water for injection (WFI) is a sterile, pharmaceutically grade of pyrogen free water.

CHAPTER 9

1. An injection is a device used for injecting a liquid, commonly a medication, into a human body with a syringe and needle.
2. Drugs are given in injectable form either to prevent drug alteration or to enhance absorption of drugs which are not absorbed in GIT.
3. Ascorbic acid is used to treat deficiency of vitamin C or scurvy.
4. Ascorbic acid (vitamin c) is usually administered orally but when oral administration is not feasible then, the drug is administered IM, IV, or subcutaneously.
5. Water for injection is sterile high-quality water prepared either by distillation or reverse osmosis or post ultra-filtration to eliminate endotoxins and pyrogens, used to deliver drug intravenously.
6. These substances are added to increase the stability or quality of the product.
7. A solution with same osmotic pressure as blood serum is said to be isotonic. For parenteral preparation, isotonicity is crucial because it lowers the chance of the product piercing into the red blood cell and inducing hemolysis. Red blood cell shrinkage will occur in a

hypertonic solution, and hemolysis will take place in a hypotonic solution.

8. Examples of Tonicity adjuster/modifier are Glycerin, lactose, mannitol, dextrose, NaCl, sodium sulfate and sorbitol

CHAPTER 10

1. Dilute sulphuric acid is used to adjust the pH of preparation because atropine sulphate is stable in acidic pH. Above pH 6 hydrolysis of atropine starts and produce turbidity in the solution and below pH 3.5 it may cause eye irritation.
2. Medicament, buffering agent, viscosity agent, antioxidants, and tonicity contributor.
3. It should be sterile, isotonic to the lachrymal secretion and free from foreign particles.
4. Preservatives are the chemical compound used to prevent bacterial growth, which help in extending shelf life of pharmaceutical product. The preservatives such as benzalkonium chloride, benzododecinium bromide are commonly used because they are compatible with the other ingredients and remain effective throughout the shelf life of the eye drops.

CHAPTER 11

1. Zinc sulphate eye drops used as astringent and mild antiseptic.
2. Label should contain instructions such as –

   NOT FOR INJECTION.

   FOR EXTERNAL USE ONLY,

   USE WITHIN ONE MONTH AFTER OPENING.
3. The commonly container used for ophthalmic preparation are glass container with plastic dropper and plastic bottles with nozzles.
4. Better patient compliance, quick absorption, less systemic side effects.
5. Methyl paraben is used as preservative agent in the preparation.
6. Drug, preservative, viscosity enhancer, buffer, isotonic agents.

7. The viscosity of eye drops determines the size of the drop and where it resides in the eye. Common viscosity enhancers include hydroxypropyl methylcellulose, polyvinyl alcohol, and methylcellulose. In order to keep the drug's comfort, solubility, stability, and activity in balance, the buffer should be added. Monobasic sodium phosphate and boric acid are common eye drop buffers.
8. The preservative used in opthalmic preparation includes Benzalkonium chloride, Chlorbutanol, Phenylmercuric acetate, Phenylmercuric nitrate.
9. Pink eye and conjunctivitis are two examples of bacterial eye diseases that can be treated with zinc sulpha eye drop. It helps reduce ocular irritation or itching and inhibits the growth of microorganisms that cause infections.

CHAPTER 12

1. These paraffins are used to relieve dryness and irritation of eye. They also moisten and lubricate the surface of the eye and act as emollient agent.
2. Wool fat is used as base in eye ointment preparation which provide a moistening film on the surface of eyeball and reduce eye irritation.
3. Eye ointment is the topical semisolid sterile ophthalmic preparation used to treat eye. infections like dry eye, conjunctivitis.
4. Conjunctivitis is an eye problem in which redness, inflammation and irritation of eyes occur due to allergies or bacteria or virus. It is also called as “pink eye” infection.

CHAPTER 13

1. Creams are less viscous than ointments due to ratio of water to oil, ointments contain roughly 80 percent oil, whereas creams contain equal amounts of water and oil. Other than that, creams having lighter, smooth texture and absorbed quickly into the skin.
2. Liquid paraffin is used as lubricating agent.
3. Cold cream is an emulsion of water-in-oil that contains fat (beeswax), mineral oil and water, prepared to moisturize the skin.

4. An emulsion is a mixture of two or more liquids that are immiscible to each other, where one of them is dispersed as small droplets in the other.
5. An emulsifying agent (also called as emulsifiers or emulgents) is a chemical compound which helps in mixing of two or more immiscible liquids and provide stability to the emulsion.

Chapter 14

1. Methyl paraben and propyl paraben in the vanishing cream are added as preservative in the ratio of (9:1).
2. Vanishing cream is the o/w type emulsion, which is applied over the skin as an emollient, which helps in moistening the skin.
3. Triethanolamine is used as an emulsifying agent and maintains the pH of the cream.
4. Lecithin, Dioceyl, Glycerin monostearate and alkali are the substitutes and commonly used in place of triethanolamine.
5. Humectant as excipient used to hydrate or moisturize the skin by pulling water from environment and deeper skin layer. Glycerin and sorbitol are common humectants.
6. Alkali, like potassium hydroxide, sodium hydroxide, is added to produce fine texture and consistency to the cream.

Chapter 15

1. 1. Protect the content from environmental hazard (light, moisture, temperature, microorganisms).
   2. Prevent loss of content from physical and thermal shock.
   3. Provide an elegant appearance to the formulation.
   4. Withstand the temperature and pressure during sterilization and transport.
2. Colorants are used in glass containers to prevent oxidation of light sensitive formulations.
3. 1. **Amber Color glass container-** It contains carbon, Sulphur or iron and manganese.

2. **Blue color glass container-** It contains cobalt and copper.
3. **Green color glass container-** It contains chromium, iron and manganese.

4. This test is used to determine the amount of alkali leaches from the surface of glass container.
5. Hydrolysis resistance is the ability of glass container to withstand the exposure of humidity and heat during storage period.
6. Packaging may be defined as the science and art which prepares the formulation for transport, storage, identification, and use.
7. Package that holds the product is called primary packaging. Boxes or containers used to hold particular amounts of primary items are considered secondary packing. Pallets and big transport containers for warehousing and storing are examples of tertiary packing.

www.ingramcontent.com/pod-product-compliance
Lightning Source LLC
Chambersburg PA
CBHW071225230926
51849CB00001B/29
9789349562240